# GOD SAVE THE QUEEN

Dennis Altman first came to attention with his book
*Homosexual: oppression & liberation* in 1972. His
recent books include *Global Sex, Gore Vidal's America*,
and *Unrequited Love: diary of an accidental activist*.
Dennis is a professorial fellow at La Trobe University
in Melbourne. He has been Visiting Professor of
Australian Studies at Harvard, and was listed by *The
Bulletin* as one of the 100 most influential Australians.

# GOD Save THE Queen

*the strange persistence of monarchies*

# DENNIS ALTMAN

SCRIBE

*Melbourne · London*

Scribe Publications
18–20 Edward St, Brunswick, Victoria 3056, Australia
2 John St, Clerkenwell, London, WC1N 2ES, United Kingdom
3754 Pleasant Ave, Suite 100, Minneapolis, Minnesota 55409, USA

Published by Scribe 2021

Typeset in Garamond Premier Pro by the publishers

Printed and bound in the UK by CPI Group (UK) Ltd,
Croydon CR0 4YY

Scribe is committed to the sustainable use of natural resources and
the use of paper products made responsibly from those resources.

978 1 950354 98 6 (US edition)
978 1 922310 56 9 (Australian edition)
978 1 913348 62 5 (UK edition)
978 1 925938 9 75 (ebook)

Catalogue records for this book are available from the National
Library of Australia and the British Library.

scribepublications.com
scribepublications.com.au
scribepublications.co.uk

# Contents

*Introduction*                                                    *1*

What is a constitutional monarchy?                          9
Monarchy and colonialism                                     18
Reviving the monarchy?                                        24
Royals as celebrities                                          28
Institutions matter                                            39
Royal fluffery: do we really need a Princess
    Michael of Kent?                      51
The dominions                                                  68
Getting rid of the Queen: the failed
    Australian republican movement        73
The Commonwealth                                               79
The Europeans                                                  84
Spain and the transition to democracy                     88
The Scandinavians and *The King's Choice*                    93
The Benelux countries                                          97
Asian monarchies                                              102
Transitional monarchies                                       117

Why do they survive?                      122
Do we need a head of state at all?        136
A final note                              142

*Acknowledgements*                        *145*
*Notes*                                   *147*

# *Introduction*

One of my earliest childhood memories is of my father waking me on 7 February 1952 to tell me that the king was dead. At primary school we were taken to watch the film of Queen Elizabeth's coronation, and when she toured Australia in early 1954 we stood for hours in the grounds of Hobart's Government House to grab a glimpse of the royal couple. The history I learnt at school and at university in Tasmania in the 1960s placed inordinate emphasis on the fate of British monarchs.

My initial enthusiasm for royal pageantry soon vanished as I became more politically aware. Monarchy, if I thought about it, seemed to me a relic of a previous world that had no place in a democratic society. When Australia held a referendum on whether to become a republic in 1999, I voted yes enthusiastically, and shared the disappointment at its failure. Today, I would vote yes again, mainly because of the absurdity of having a head of state who is sovereign of a foreign country.

Over the past century large numbers of monarchies, have collapsed, including those of major powers such as China, Russia, and Germany, and only a few new ones have come into being. This would suggest that, in the face of increasing demands for democratisation, the very idea of monarchy is likely to disappear. When he was deposed in Egypt in 1952, King Farouk predicted that there would be five monarchs left at the end of the century: the kings of hearts, diamonds, clubs, spades, and of England.[1] To date, his prediction has proved wrong, although discontent with monarchy appears to be growing in several countries, notably Spain and Thailand. While the twentieth century saw the collapse of monarchies across Europe, many democratic societies have retained monarchical systems, and there are well-organised supporters of monarchical restoration in Romania, Serbia, and Georgia.

Monarchies are expensive, extravagant, a remnant of feudalism, bastions of privilege, and symbols of inherited power. On the face of it, they are anachronisms, deeply antithetic to democratic principles. Yet before we dismiss the institution as the bastion of right-wing fantasies, it's worth noting that, on balance, those countries that have developed constitutional monarchies rank among the most democratic and egalitarian: the Scandinavian and Benelux states all have hereditary heads of state. In Asia the picture varies: Japan, Malaysia, and Thailand are constitutional monarchies, although the political role of the monarch in Thailand is such that, rather like in Jordan and Morocco, it is not clear whether it should be classified as a constitutional monarchy. In Spain, after the death of Franco in 1975 and the restoration of the monarchy, King Juan Carlos played a crucial role in the establishment of parliamentary government.

Over forty countries have retained monarchies in the twenty-first century. With a few exceptions, such as in Saudi Arabia or Brunei, absolute monarchies have disappeared, although there are a number of monarchies that I term transitional, in which power is shared uneasily between hereditary and elected officials. Outside the Arab world the majority of monarchs today wield little power and play a largely symbolic role, representing an apolitical and idealised image of the nation. These, as we learn in introductory civics lessons, are constitutional monarchies.

There is a large literature comparing presidential and parliamentary systems, but little of it questions the difference between systems with appointed versus hereditary heads of state. Leftists want to overthrow hereditary rule; the right wants to venerate it. Over twenty years ago, two American political scientists, Jeremy Mayer and Lee Sigelman, demonstrated that there was a correlation between monarchy and various measures of societal well-being and wealth:

> According to data collected, having a monarch adds $3619.43 per capita each year to a nation's gross domestic product — many times the annual budget for the wages

of liveried footmen, the purchase of new polo mallets, the dry-cleaning of ermine robes and the other essentials of the royal lifestyle.[2]

I first came across their article in the truly bizarre publications of *The International Commission on Nobility and Royalty* [sic], which cited it without any recognition of irony.

Constitutional monarchy remains a remarkably under-researched area of comparative politics: there are few serious attempts to compare existing monarchies across Asia and Europe. (Peter Conradi's very gossipy *Great Survivors* is confined to Europe.) Lèse-majesté laws in Thailand, Morocco, and Malaysia are used to prevent any criticism of the monarchy, and perhaps a key characteristic of constitutional monarchy is the freedom it provides to criticise the royal family. Less draconian laws in Spain did not prevent the uncovering of major scandals around King Juan Carlos, and informal agreements to keep royal indiscretions well hidden have largely collapsed in our age of twenty-four-hour electronic media.

Looking at constitutional monarchies across the world gives us a new perspective on our all-too-familiar picture of the British monarchy. The English-speaking world knows relatively little about non-British royals, except when someone from the Anglosphere — such as Grace Kelly in Monaco or Mary Donaldson in Denmark — marries up. But all hereditary rulers share the dilemma summed up by Craig Brown in his excoriating portrait of Princess Margaret: 'Born in an age of deference, the Princess was to die in an age of egalitarianism.'[3] After all, if the royals become like everyone else, what is the point of having them? But if they remain aloof, how do they maintain popular support?

Why bother, as several people asked me when I explained this project. Like Pimlott, I became interested in the continuing existence of monarchy, and was increasingly drawn to exploring an institution that persists in societies as different as Norway, Lesotho, and Japan. Ben Pimlott, the Fabian socialist whose biography of Elizabeth I is perhaps the best book yet written on the modern British monarchy, wrote that his interest in the subject was piqued by the reality that, '[a]n institution and a family dismissed by the sophisticated as trivial and irrelevant was nevertheless the subject of fascinated analysis, humour and comment'.[4]

Concepts of royalty are deeply embedded in the popular imagination, even in countries that have long ago abolished monarchical rule. We grow up with fairy stories that embody concepts of royalty: *Cinderella* is possibly the most popular of all such stories, with counterparts in many cultures, and images of royalty suffuse popular culture. Surprising numbers of autocratic states encourage the study of royal history to establish their legitimacy. The Russian Revolution saw the bloody assassination of the tsar and his immediate family, but in 2000 the Russian Orthodox Church canonised Nicholas II and his family, and in recent years hundreds of books and films about the Romanovs have been released. The mythical Chinese Yellow Emperor, who is claimed to have originated the centralised Chinese state, is now invoked by communist leaders to justify Beijing's control over its extended territory, including Tibet, and its claims for Taiwan. (The last Chinese emperor, Puyi, abdicated in 1912, but was restored as emperor of the Japanese province of Manchuria in 1934, then imprisoned by the Chinese government and eventually 'rehabilitated' as a supporter of the communist government.)

I began this book intrigued by the possibility that constitutional monarchy might be a bulwark against the worst sort of populist authoritarianism, curious whether a study of existing monarchies might help our understanding of contemporary political developments. The apparent triumph of liberal democracy after the collapse of the Berlin Wall and the Soviet Union has given way to a number of regimes that the Hungarian prime minister, Viktor Orbán, termed 'illiberal democracy'. Orbán is one of a number of political rulers who have greatly expanded their constitutional powers to resemble those of absolute monarchs: one thinks of Putin in Russia, Erdoğan in Turkey, Maduro in Venezuela, and, although less successful in exerting total control, Bolsonaro in Brazil and Modi in India. Donald Trump was clearly fascinated by such strongmen — and they are all men — but the United States retained sufficient checks to prevent him from emulating them, while Xi

Jinping in China presides over an unapologetically one-party state.

It is striking that none of these countries is among the thirty or so constitutional monarchies that exist today: are constitutional monarchies an antidote to the worst excesses of populist politicians? In an era of growing authoritarian and populist leaders, constitutional monarchs, who are perceived as standing above partisan politics, look increasingly attractive. Much as we might deplore the undemocratic nature of monarchy, is it less damaging than the illiberal forms of democracy now on the rise globally? If we crave 'bread and circuses', the perpetuation of royal sagas may be less harmful than the fantasies of autocratic rulers.

If a certain sort of authoritarian machismo seems on the rise globally, so too are demands for greater accountability and participation. Despite a global COVID-19 pandemic, the year 2020 saw major demonstrations for democratisation in countries as varied as Belarus, Lebanon, and Hong Kong — and, most relevant to the themes of this book, Thailand.

Writing about politics is always fraught; events can change what seemed certainties in the period between writing and publication. Even where it seems entrenched, monarchy needs to reinvent itself to remain relevant; in the course of writing this book, there were major challenges to the King of Thailand, continuing scandals around the royal families of Belgium, Britain, and Spain, and political uncertainties in Malaysia that required the intervention of the king. Even in an era of constitutional monarchy, the person who holds the throne can be significant in determining whether the institution survives or crumbles.

# What is a constitutional monarchy?

In 1889, the new Swedish Social Democratic Party called for the establishment of a republic. Well over a century later, Sweden retains a king as head of state — although, like the Emperor of Japan, one shorn of any residual political power. Sweden and Japan are the best current examples of monarchies for whom any exercise of royal political power is expressly forbidden. Like almost all monarchs, they hold their position through inheritance rather than any process of election, although in some countries the monarch is selected from members of the ruling families.

In broad terms, a constitutional monarchy is one where the monarch is head of state, while effective power is in the hands of a government responsible to a freely elected parliament. This is a somewhat more restrictive definition than the one that includes any country in which the sovereign exercises authority in accordance with a written or unwritten constitution, which might include countries in which the monarch still exercises dominant political power. Here I am drawing on the work of political theorist Karl Popper, for whom the acid test of democracy was 'whether bad rulers can be got rid of without bloodshed, without violence'.[1] As Adam Gopnik wrote, 'Prime Ministers, when they become unpopular, are eased out by their supporters; kings, when they become unpopular, must be thrown out by a mob.'[2] In a constitutional monarchy an unpopular king could ultimately be removed by the parliament, or possibly by a popular referendum.

It is not accidental that the concept of state sovereignty and the sovereign as an absolute ruler share the same word. The term was originated by the philosopher Jean Bodin to bolster the role of the French King Henry III in the sixteenth century. Originally, sovereignty, as the word implies, was vested in a monarch who claimed absolute power, often through divine providence or, indeed, descent from the gods, as was believed of the Japanese emperor. Several Habsburg emperors claimed descent from Noah and other Old Testament figures. Various forms of absolute monarchical rule could be found in societies as different as Babylon, Sri Lanka, the Aztec Empire (in what is now Mexico), and African kingdoms such as the Empire of Benin.[3] In the West, our dominant image of monarchy dates from the consolidation of nation-states by powerful rulers such as Louis XIV and Catherine the Great, who both eliminated feudal power structures while perpetuating ideas of hereditary status. Monarchs became expressions of national identity, as suggested in the language of Shakespeare's *Henry V*, but it was not until the eighteenth century that defining nations in terms of monarchical realms gave way to one based upon what Benedict Anderson famously called 'imagined communities'.

In Europe, claims that sovereignty rests in the people, normally expressed through an elected parliament, led to constant conflict between monarchs and their populations, most dramatically in the executions of Charles I in Britain (in 1649) and Louis XVI in France (1793). In Britain, the monarchy was revived, although Charles's son, James II, was in turn deposed in 1688 and replaced by his reliably Protestant daughter Mary and her husband, William of Orange. The basic assumptions of constitutional monarchy emerged out of the century of conflict between monarch and a rising middle class in Britain; James's second daughter, Queen Anne, was the last British sovereign to veto a bill passed by parliament, and successive monarchs acceded, though not without some resistance, to the idea that political power grew out of parliamentary majorities. British monarchs might well have been following Machiavelli's advice in *The Prince*: 'All a monarch need do is avoid upsetting the order established by his predecessors, trim policies to circumstances when there is trouble, and, assuming he is of average ability, he will keep his kingdom for life.'

In France, following a period of republican rule, Napoleon Bonaparte proclaimed himself emperor in 1804 as the embodiment of the nation rather than through divine appointment; after his defeat in 1815, France experienced several monarchical restorations, ending with the fall of Napoleon III in 1870 and the creation of a third republic. The French Revolution followed the break from Britain by her American colonies, and the combined influence of the French and American revolutions meant monarchs would increasingly need to argue that their legitimacy came from the people rather than from divine providence. For people discontented with autocratic rule, republicanism presented an alternative model, one that would be adopted by most of the former colonies of South and Central America.

When new states were created in Europe in the last century it was assumed a monarch was required, and there were many surplus princes available. The slow collapse of the Ottoman Empire saw monarchies established across the Balkans, often by princelings plucked from the ample stores of the German Empire. After gaining its independence from Turkey in 1912, Albania was gifted a German prince by the Great Powers, but his reign was very short-lived; later, in 1928, the Albanian president declared himself King Zog, but his reign was effectively ended by Italian occupation. In the bitter civil war that accompanied Finnish independence from Russia in 1918, there were suggestions for establishing a monarchy; a Hessian prince was chosen, but he renounced the throne without ever coming to Finland. Similarly, in 1918, newly independent Lithuania proclaimed the German Duke Wilhelm as king; he accepted and took the name Mindaugas II, but within six months the monarchy was dissolved. Wilhelm had previously held hopes of ascending to the throne of either Monaco or Albania. After the collapse of the Ottoman Empire, the British, who had mandates from the League of Nations to govern parts of the former Ottoman Empire, created monarchies for the Hashemite family in both Jordan and Iraq; King Faisal of Iraq was killed in the revolution of 1958, but King Abdullah II is the great grandson of the first monarch of Jordan. A few years later, Reza Khan, a former army officer, established himself as the Shah of Iran, replacing the former dynasty.

Most overthrowals of monarchies occur through revolution — such as in France, Russia, Iran, and China — or as a consequence of war. The defeat of Germany and Austria-Hungary in World War I, and the revolution in Russia sparked by that war, meant the end not only of three imperial monarchies, but also of a period in which interlocking royal families seemed to control most of Europe. The rulers of Britain, Germany, and Russia were cousins, but they found themselves on opposing sides; and even though Russia and Britain were allies, the British government, apparently with the full acquiescence of George V, refused sanctuary to the tsar and his family, who were subsequently shot. George also changed the name of his dynasty to Windsor, to disguise its strongly Germanic ancestry. The Ottoman Empire had allied with Germany, and its collapse meant the end of a six-hundred-year-old dynasty, to be replaced by what is now Turkey and large sections of the

Middle East that came under British and French control.

After World War II, Greece abolished and restored the monarchy several times, most recently in 1974 when a referendum opposed a return of the monarchy following the end of military rule. Italy voted in a referendum in 1946 to abolish the monarchy, and King Victor Emmanuel took refuge with King Farouk in Egypt, who in turn would be overthrown in 1952 — and flee to Italy. In the years following the independence of India and Pakistan in 1947, most former British colonies abolished the monarchy on gaining independence. It seems far easier to get rid of monarchies than to invent them, although in a few cases, such as in Cambodia and Spain, popular votes have restored monarchies.

Historically, monarchies have survived by surrendering political power in the face of rising demands for participation and elected governments. The American political scientist Samuel Huntington wrote of 'the King's dilemma', whereby the monarch could either 'attempt to maintain his authority by continuing to modernize but intensify the repression necessary to keep control', or move towards a constitutional monarchy where 'the king reigns but does not rule'. It is believed that Edward VII advised his nephew Tsar Nicholas II to do just that — advice that Nicholas ignored. Even when mass protests forced him to accept some form of elected assembly in 1905, Nicholas resisted, believing it was 'harmful to the people whom God has entrusted to his care'.

Huntington wrote his major study in 1968, focused

on countries in what American political scientists liked to term 'the developing world'. He identified ten monarchies then grappling with the demands of modernisation.[4] Since then, the monarchies have collapsed in half of them — Afghanistan, Ethiopia, Iran, Libya, and Nepal — and only Saudi Arabia remains as an absolute monarchy. Already in 1968, Huntington pointed to Morocco, where King Hassan was instituting a political liberalisation, although Morocco today is far from a fully constitutional monarchy.

Most interesting is the case of Iran, where Huntington identified tensions arising from the Shah's determination to maintain power, sometimes in opposition to the elected parliament. After the overthrowal of the Mossadegh government with the backing of the CIA in 1953, the Shah became increasingly dependent upon American support and a brutal secret police, resisting any real development of democratic rule, which he claimed was impossible in Iran. He is reported to have said, 'When the Iranians learn to behave like Swedes, I will behave like the King of Sweden.'[5] Ten years after Huntington wrote, a revolution forced the Shah to flee, and installed an Islamic regime. Had Pahlavi shown more faith in the Iranian people, he might have been able to save his dynasty. The present King of Thailand seems bent on ignoring historical lessons in demanding increased political power while flaunting accepted morality; it is difficult to see his reign ending well.

It is striking that all those countries with genuine constitutional monarchies are wealthy, even if some of the wealthiest countries in the world — such as Brunei and Qatar — remain under absolute monarchical rule. The transition from autocratic to constitutional monarchy is most likely when there is sufficient wealth to create a large and educated middle class who adopt the norms of Western liberal democracy, but it also depends on the actions of the monarchs themselves. There are more examples of monarchs who failed to make this transition than there are of successes.

Some absolute monarchies remain, primarily in the Middle East, although one might regard the Papacy as an elected monarchy. Outside the Middle East, monarchies remain largely as symbolic holders of sovereignty without real powers. There remain some small principalities where hereditary rulers hold significant powers, such as Monaco, Liechtenstein, and Bhutan; but in Scandinavia, Benelux, Spain, Malaysia, Japan, and the British dominions, the monarchy is essentially the symbolic holder of sovereignty. While most Commonwealth countries are republics, the Queen remains head of state in fifteen, most of them small island countries. As far as I know, Bhutan is the only country with formal provisions for forcing the monarch to abdicate, along with a compulsory retirement age of sixty-five. Abdication is more common than many Britons realise — in 2013, the rulers of Belgium, Qatar, and the Netherlands all stood down, along with Pope Benedict — but it usually occurs after long periods on the throne. Since Sweden abolished male primogeniture in 1980, most constitutional monarchies have allowed the throne to pass to the eldest child, regardless of gender.

Despite massive social changes, royalty remains based on nineteenth-century assumptions around nation and family, and, to a lesser extent, religion. Traditionally, monarchs claimed their authority came from the gods — the divine right of kings — a position that would seem incompatible with any notion of democratic rule, but the links to official religion remain. In Britain and Denmark, the monarch remains the nominal head of an established church, and the Norwegian monarch is required to adhere to the Lutheran Church of Norway. The Malaysian king is recognised as 'head of Islam', while the Thai king is regarded as both semi-sacred and a protector of Buddhism, a tendency that was deliberately cultivated during the long reign of King Bhumipol. The King of Morocco is officially recognised as Commander of the Faithful, and the Malaysian sultans are recognised as having a role in defending Islam.

# Monarchy and colonialism

Starting with Spanish and Portuguese ventures across the Atlantic and Indian oceans in the sixteenth century, European monarchies and trading companies embarked on overseas ventures fuelled by the desire for trade and political control. Inevitably, this led to bloody clashes with local rulers, as in the Spanish wars against the Aztec and Inca empires.

Early European ambitions in Africa meant a need to ally with local rulers; at the end of the fifteenth century, the Portuguese supported King Álvaro of the Kongo, who pledged allegiance to the Portuguese king in return for assistance against local rivals.[1]

By the end of the nineteenth century, European countries had expanded their control over much of the rest of the world through colonial enterprises supported by monarchs, who often took a personal interest — such as Queen Victoria's fascination with India in later life. Victoria's supremacy was recognised with the title of Empress of India in 1876, a title not abandoned by her successors until Indian independence. (Judy Dench, who has played several British monarchs in her acting career, has made a film, *Victoria and Abdul*, centred on Victoria's relationship with her Indian servant, who taught her some Hindi.) The lack of a monarch after 1870 did not, however, slow the French government in seeking the expansion of its overseas territories.

Much of British and Dutch expansion into south and south-east Asia was driven by commercial rather than royal interests; but in Africa, Belgium's King Leopold made the Congo his own personal preserve, and was responsible for millions of deaths in his exploitation of the ivory and rubber trades. Germany's Kaiser Wilhelm was directly implicated in the massacres that accompanied German colonisation of South West Africa (now Namibia). Widespread European colonisation undermined traditional monarchical systems across the global south, although colonial rulers often chose to exert power through existing royalty, as in the case of Britain's recognition of Indian principalities, or the role of the Emperor of Annam within French Indio-China. In other cases, such as the American annexation of Hawaii or the French conquest of Madagascar, ruling dynasties were swept aside.

The British Raj maintained a patchwork of subordinate states in which the traditional rulers followed the advice of a British resident; at the end of British rule, 565 princely states were officially recognised in the Indian subcontinent, governing almost one-quarter of the total population. The new governments of India and Pakistan were not inclined to accept these divisions. After Indian independence in 1947, there were moves in the princely states of Travancore and Hyderabad to become independent monarchies, but these moves were suppressed by the new government of India. Under Indira Gandhi's government, an amendment to the Indian constitution in 1971 'terminated the privy purses and privileges of the Rulers of former Indian States'. Indian princes still have considerable social prestige — as demonstrated, for example, by the high profile of the heir to the Maharaja of Rajpipla, who is an active crusader for queer rights. But the days when the Nizam of Hyderabad was reputedly the richest man in the world are now past.

Anti-colonial movements meant the repudiation of European monarchy, although there were significant exceptions, as in the establishment of a Brazilian empire for most of the nineteenth century. In New Zealand, Māori resistance to white settlers led to the creation of a Māori monarchy (Kingitanga) in 1858, with the hope that it could unite the Māori population to assist in dealing with the British authorities. Although without recognition in New Zealand's constitution, the position remains and has been inherited by six descendants of the first king, Potatau Te Wherowhero. Queen Te Atairangikaahu held the position for forty years (1966–2006) and became a highly respected figure in the country.

In some cases, traditional rulers became key figures in the struggle for independence, as was the case for Prince Sihanouk in Cambodia. In the mid-twentieth century, Morocco's King Mohammed V became identified with the independence movement and was briefly deposed by the French, returning to negotiate Moroccan independence in 1957.

George Washington rejected the idea of an American king, and revolutions in the Americas ended the belief that a king was needed to embody the sense of national identity, although the largest of the former South American colonies, Brazil, to where the Portuguese king had fled Napoleon in 1808, became independent under the crown prince, the Emperor Dom Pedro, and remained a monarchy for sixty-seven years. Haiti had three different but short-lived monarchies after winning independence in 1804, and for several brief periods in the nineteenth century Mexico was a monarchy, first under independence leader Agustin de Iturbide, and later under the Habsburg Maximillian, who was installed by the French in 1864 and executed three years later when the Mexican republic was restored. With the end of colonialism, few African or Asian states sought to establish monarchies, although, in former French Indo-China, kings were installed in Laos and Cambodia after independence. The Laotian monarchy was abolished after the victory of the Pathet Lao in 1975; the Cambodian monarchy was abolished by a coup in 1970 and restored in 1993.

In many parts of Asia and Africa, traditional rulers still retain considerable cultural and religious significance, as is true for the Sultan of Sokoto or the Emir of Kano in Nigeria. The South African constitution recognises the existence and authority of traditional rulers, but does not give them sovereignty. Nonetheless, certain rulers such as King Goodwill of the Zulu Nation have at times clashed with the central government. Ethiopia took its modern form in the mid-nineteenth century, and resisted European colonisation until the occupation by Italy between 1935 and 1941; after that, Emperor Haile Selassie returned to the throne, to be overthrown by a military revolt in 1974. The Ethiopian dynasty claims descent from King Solomon and the Queen of Sheba, and still has support from some religious Ethiopians.

In Indonesia, where the Dutch colonialists had retained a certain number of traditional rulers, the Sultan of Yogyakarta managed to maintain power through both Japanese occupation and independence, becoming vice-president of the country while retaining his position as governor of the region. A referendum in 2012 ratified his son in the unique position of hereditary governor of the Yogyakarta special region. The current sultan, Hamengkubuwono X, has upset traditionalists by naming his eldest daughter as his heir, and has been prominent in bringing together former traditional rulers across Indonesia. Even if they are without formal power, princely families still have influence and prestige.

If European monarchies recall their imperial glories, they can also evoke uneasy memories of conquest, exploitation, and slavery. In 2013, King Philippe of Belgium expressed 'profound regrets' for the wounds inflicted on the Congo under its brutal colonial rule, and the Dutch king Willem-Alexander apologised for 'excessive violence' in a visit to Indonesia in 2020. On a visit to Ghana in 2018, Prince Charles apologised for the 'appalling atrocity of the slave trade', and the current and previous Japanese emperors have acknowledged brutality and war crimes in their occupation of Korea and China. But the palaces and museums of London, Brussels, and Madrid are constant reminders of the ways in which colonial wealth was accumulated. There will probably be increasing pressure for royal families to publicly acknowledge this history; in 2019, the Mexican president requested the Pope and the Spanish king apologise for the massacres and oppression of the Spanish conquest.

# Reviving the monarchy?

Monarchist movements exist in a range of countries, although in most cases as no more than fringe groups caught up in nostalgia for an imagined past. Monarchists of all sorts existed in inter-war Europe, including groups such as the German Social Monarchists, who sought the return of the Kaiser, but as the head of a 'workers' state'. Oddest, perhaps, is the report in 2016 that a majority of Brazilians would like a restoration of the monarchy, which was abolished in 1889 but still has a pretender in the wings. There are a number of such pretenders, most of whom are figures of fun rather than serious political players, but there is some support for a monarchical revival among right-wing Brazilians.

There are French monarchists who engage in absurd squabbles over who has the best claim for a throne that no longer exists, and there is equal arguing among putative heirs to the Italian throne. In Turkey, there is renewed interest in the former Ottoman imperial family, President Erdoğan having reversed a century of republican secularism with an Islamic nationalism that embraces the Ottoman heritage. There is a small monarchist movement in Russia, which attracts authoritarian and anti-Semitic nationalists; the putative Romanov heir, Grand Duchess Maria Vladimirovna, has some support from the Russian Orthodox Church. And there is lingering support for monarchy even in countries where republicanism seems entrenched. Germany abolished its monarchy after the defeat of World War I; yet, a century later, the Hohenzollern family is still pressing its claims to royal property, and there are figures on the right of German politics who look back nostalgically to their reign.[1] There is an annual monarchist march in Prague, calling for a return of the Habsburg throne; nostalgia for the Habsburgs appears to exist across most of the various countries that made up part of the Austro-Hungarian Empire.

In the realm of fantasy, one can find Jacobites who claim that the throne of Scotland belongs by right to the Duke of Bavaria, a descendent of the Stuart kings, whose claims were displaced by an insistence on a Protestant monarch for Great Britain.

The claims of one of Haile Selassie's grandsons to the Ethiopian throne were supported by some members of the US House of Representatives after a visit by Prince Ermias to Washington in 1999. Republican congressman Jim Saxton argued that the prince 'exemplified the capable, unifying symbolism that Ethiopia desperately needs'.[2] A small movement of Ethiopian exiles argue that a constitutional monarchy would prevent the bitter descent into tribalism that has characterised Ethiopian politics, echoing Abraham Lincoln in their claim that '[w]e are of the people, by the people and with the people, we will restore the Ethiopian monarchy in a constitutional framework in order to restore hope for all Ethiopians and accountability for those who govern us'.[3] Some members of the royal family appear to have directed their efforts into business and cultural projects within Ethiopia. There are several monarchist groups active amongst Iranian exiles, and the Iranian government has accused monarchists of responsibility for several terrorist bombings.

It is unlikely that one could invent a monarchy from scratch, although the foibles of many authoritarian leaders match those of most royals, and at least one, President Bokassa of the Central African Republic, crowned himself emperor in 1976, and kept control until he was overthrown in a French-assisted coup several years later. Only fringe groups, almost always on the extreme right, talk of creating new monarchies, as in the case of the Moon Family's Sanctuary Church, whose leaders speak of instituting 'a libertarian Christian monarchy' in the United States.

Even where monarchy has been abolished, royal families may continue to play a semi-official role representing their country, as is the case of Duarte Pio, Duke of Braganza and pretender to the Portuguese throne. Dom

Duarte is significant because he was a strong defender of East Timor's independence against Indonesia and was awarded Timorese citizenship in recognition of his support for the cause. Timor had been a Portuguese colony, and the duke presumably felt some loyalty to people who would previously have been his subjects. In Montenegro, which was an independent kingdom until it was annexed by Serbia, there is official recognition of the royal family, who are given certain ceremonial functions and the use of the royal palace.

# Royals as celebrities

The historian Martyn Rady has claimed that monarchs were the first modern celebrities: 'They were objects of spectacle, whose image was through the photograph and mass-produced engraving made into a commodity that lent them a "larger than life" quality.'[1] By the time of the Habsburg Emperor Franz Joseph's sixtieth anniversary on the throne, ashtrays, aprons, and daguerreotypes of the emperor circulated throughout Austria-Hungary.

In today's world of internet and twenty-four-hour news cycles, royals provide endless fodder for media gossip, forcing several families to seek legal protection against paparazzi — as the Netherlands Crown Prince Willem-Alexander did in 2009, and Prince Harry did in 2019. But while royals complain about intrusions on their privacy, theirs is a co-dependent relationship: royal families know that their continuing privileges depend upon media access. Autocratic monarchies seek to protect their public image, as in the endless footage of official royal ceremonies on Thai television, but elsewhere the smallest detail of royal behaviour is fodder for press, television, and social media. I once read ten pages in *Hola!*, Spain's celebrity magazine, in which the Queen's trip to the ballet with her two daughters was hailed as the most consequential event of the week. In Belgium and the Netherlands there are regular television programs devoted to royal gossip, while the French magazine *Paris Match* has a regular royal blog, which seems particularly fond of the British and Monegasque families. Denmark's Queen Margrethe is probably the most open of current monarchs, and collaborated in a book about her life in which she manages to present herself as simultaneously one of the people and yet destined to reign.[2]

It is tempting to speak of monarchies as part of celebrity culture, whereby royal families become familiar characters in national soap operas, reassuring their audience precisely because they appear untouched by the grubbiness of political intrigue, even if their propensity for scandalous personal behaviour challenges that of Hollywood. Yet, in a very perceptive article, Arianne Chernock argues that it is a mistake to just see royalty as 'an entertaining diversion ... It endures because it also shapes contemporary politics and sensibilities, giving air to social anxieties and lending legitimacy to preferences and practices from households to industry in Britain and beyond.'[3] Because they symbolise a nation, royals are accorded celebrity status irrespective of their personal attributes.

Considerable efforts are made to maintain members of the monarchy in the public eye as symbols of the nation. It is not accidental that royal weddings and births are subject to enormous scrutiny. Because the monarchy is a continuing family saga, it creates emotional connections with its subjects that continue despite the bad behaviour of individual royals. Monarchy depends upon the concept of a family passed on through generations, so that royal births, deaths, and marriages are central to their mystique. Unlike politicians, we assume royalty remains through our lifetime. As Jeremy Paxman puts it, 'Monarchy replicates the human condition in a way that politics does not.'[4] Of course, who constitutes the royal family is itself open to dispute, as was evident in the 2020 court case in which the illegitimate daughter of the former King Albert of Belgium won recognition as a princess and member of the royal house.

As royalty increasingly marries outside its extended families, it becomes a pathway to sudden lifetime celebrity, as in the case of commoners such as Mary Donaldson in Denmark or Kate Middleton in Britain, who married heirs to the throne. The increasing tendency of royals to marry commoners reinforces the myth of monarchy as transcending the realities of class, even beyond such egalitarian settings as Oslo and Amsterdam. There are fewer examples of male commoners becoming royal through marriage, although the future Queen of Sweden is married to her personal trainer. In a world of autocratic machismo, there may be something particularly reassuring about female monarchs; even when the sovereign is a man there is constant focus on his wife and daughters. Indeed, women have often held the throne in societies where only men were regarded as fit to enter politics, as was the case for Queen Victoria or Queen Wilhelmina, who came to the Dutch throne almost twenty years before women got the vote in the Netherlands. Wilhelmina reigned for nearly fifty-eight years, and was succeeded by her daughter and then grand-daughter; it took 123 years for the Netherlands to have a male sovereign again.

The attention paid to royal events, and the crowds that regularly turn out for royal weddings and funerals, suggests that they fulfil a need beyond their purely constitutional role. It's estimated that 750 million people worldwide watched Charles and Diana's wedding in 1981, and two billion tuned in to her funeral in 1997, although this is fewer than the most widely viewed sporting events. Millions of people identify with the continuing stories of royalty, who seem both like and different from the great majority of their 'subjects'. Nor is this only true for European royalty; the marriage of King Mohammed of Morocco in 2002 was treated as a major national event, and against previous custom his wife, the Princess Lalla Salma, became a public figure similar to European royal consorts. Her seeming disappearance from Morocco since 2018 was the subject of considerable media speculation, but two years later one could find photographs of her performing royal duties.

Presidents come and go; the attraction of monarchy is its continuity. We grow old alongside the royals, and their familial problems become as familiar as our own. As Roland Barthes observed over half a century ago, the French, despite their own history, 'pine for fresh news about royal activities, of which they are extremely fond'.[5] Barthes would presumably have enjoyed the very silly French film *Connasse, princesse des coeurs*, in which a Parisienne determines to marry Prince Harry.

Royalty may have lost political power, but, in an era of mass media and distrust of politicians, they exercise considerable 'soft power', a term devised by the American political scientist Joseph Nye as 'the ability to get what you want through attraction rather than coercion or payment [that] arises from the attractiveness of a country's culture, political ideals and policies'.[6] Perhaps because he is American, Nye initially ignored the role of monarchy in promoting soft power; in discussing potential 'soft power resources', he listed seven areas where Britain does well, but ignored the huge global following of the British royal family. Even so, Nye clearly recognised the importance of the royals, writing a piece in 2013 headed 'The infant Prince George is a source of real-world power'.[7]

Presumably, plans are already afoot to prepare George to eventually succeed his great-grandmother as sovereign. It takes considerable effort to train an heir to the throne: young princes are usually put through one form or other of military service, however unsuitable they may be. (Princess

Elizabeth, the heir to the Belgian throne, is also doing military training.) As one account of the preparations in Morocco for the eventual accession of Prince Moulay Hassan put it:

> The first step is attendance at the Royal Academy founded in 1942 by Mohammed V, where the crown prince is welcomed by classmates. There, as tradition has it, the future king receives a well-rounded education in both theology and modern academic subjects, as well as in sports and the arts, not to mention palace protocol, which includes the etiquette and rules of the royal court.[8]

The British are particularly skilled at using royal pomp to project images of power. I have a vivid memory of images from a state visit by President Lech Wałęsa of Poland in 2016, when the former president seemed dwarfed and ill at ease amidst a full roll call of the royals ushering him into a formal banquet. For small countries, a ruling dynasty can attract attention that would otherwise be difficult to generate. The long-lived Queen Sālote of Tonga gained international celebrity when she attended the coronation of Queen Elizabeth in 1953; she had already been queen for thirty-five years, and was an honorary dame in four different British orders. For several generations of people across the Empire, then the Commonwealth, she embodied Tonga. But the Tongan monarchy drew inspiration from the British: Tāufa'āhau, the chief who 'unified' the islands in the early 1800s, was baptised George (Siaosi) after George III, and his wife was baptised Charlotte (Sālote). Images of the current King Tupou VI's coronation show him dressed in the style of a British monarch.

A detailed study of royal soft power in nineteenth-century Europe demonstrated the efforts of royal families to ensure their relevance as they lost political power.[9] Public holidays, such as Koningsdag in the Netherlands, which celebrate the King's birthday, are carefully curated to enhance the image of the royal family as central to national pride. Governments will deliberately send members of their royal families to visit foreign countries as a way of promoting political and economic ties. Nor is this a recent phenomenon: in 1896, it is claimed, 900,000 spectators cheered the tsar and tsarina of Russia as they travelled through Paris.[10] As Prince of Wales, Edward VIII attracted huge crowds on tours across his future dominions.

Edward's grandfather, Edward VII, was the last British monarch to play an overtly active role in diplomacy, but both Prince Charles and Prince William have visited occupied Palestine, clearly signalling British support for a Palestinian state. And it is striking how many royals are prominent in international sporting bodies, following the lead of Crown Prince Constantine of Greece, who was crucial in the invention of the modern Olympic Games. In 2020 the admittedly large International Olympic Committee included at least nine members of royal families.

The celebrity status of royal families was summed up in Andy Warhol's boast that he wanted to be as famous as the Queen of England. In 1985 he created a series of silkscreen prints portraying four ruling queens at that time: Queen Elizabeth II of England, Queen Beatrix of Netherlands, Queen Margrethe II of Denmark, and Queen Ntombi Twala of Swaziland. Increasingly, royalty becomes indistinguishable from other global celebrities, a point made by Takashi Fujitani, who wrote of the ways in which the Japanese imperial family has been banalised into yet another commodity in consumer society.[11] But this under-estimates the continuing influence and mystique of royalty, even as their more publicised antics seem indistinguishable from that of the Kardashians. When the Queen appeared alongside Daniel Craig as James Bond in a video played at the opening of the 2012 Olympics, she followed this by appearing as sovereign at the ceremony itself.

The wedding of Prince Harry and Meghan Markle in 2018 was widely hailed as a meeting between royal tradition and Hollywood celebrity, with the added bonus that it brought someone of non-European ancestry into 'the firm'. As we now know, things didn't work out as planned, perhaps because it proved impossible to assimilate someone with an already existing celebrity status into the arcane restrictions of British royalty. Markle was understandably reluctant to succumb to the demands of royal behaviour, as fellow actress Grace Kelly had when she married Prince Rainer of Monaco in 1956.

Celebrity is largely transitory and rarely passed on beyond one generation; a celebrity can always be replaced in ways that are far more difficult in the case of a royal. And even a monarch devoid of power represents the principle of inherited entitlement, carried to absurd lengths in both Thailand and Great Britain, although not even Princess Margaret expected her servants to approach her on their knees, as is the Thai custom. But even democratically minded monarchs demand deference and are partially immune from the sort of scrutiny applied to politicians in democratic societies.

Monarchs and their heirs are expected to marry and have children, and unpopular marriages can unsettle the monarchy, as in the case of Edward VIII's abdication to marry Wallis Simpson. There were demonstrations in the Netherlands in 1966 when the heir to the throne, Princess Beatrix, married a former German officer, Claus von Amsberg, who became Prince Consort. In 2019 the Malaysian king, Yang-di Pertuan Mohammed, abdicated after reports that he had married a twenty-five-year-old former Miss Moscow. To date there are no examples of royal heirs marrying a same-sex partner, although a Belgian journalist claimed that King Philippe married to cover up a long-term homosexual affair.[12] While gay prime ministers are acceptable, at least in Belgium, Luxembourg, and even Serbia, no monarch or immediate family member is openly homosexual, although there are persistent rumours about the current Cambodian king. In 2016 three people were arrested after a photograph was featured on Facebook in which Sihamoni's face had been photoshopped onto a gay-porn image, with the words 'Cambodia King is gay' added. Given the enormous weight attached to continuing the family line, a homosexual monarch raises interesting questions about how far a monarchy could adjust to changing mores.

The apparent democratic mores of the Danish or Dutch courts don't really disguise the enormous wealth that most royal families have accumulated over generations. The statelets of Monaco and Liechtenstein are ruled by families whom *Forbes* magazine estimate as richer than the British. Following World War I, Queen Wilhelmina of the Netherlands was allegedly the richest woman in the world, and her investments were important for Dutch business. The Thai family is probably the richest of all, and the current King Vajiralongkorn has been able to transfer much of the Crown's holdings into his personal control. Gossip magazines claim that the King of Morocco has twelve palaces around the world, all perpetually kept at seventeen degrees and fully staffed, and that he will order the drive-past of a dozen expensive cars in order to choose the one that he wants for the day. Despite the wealth of these dynasties, there appear to be few notable royal philanthropists; they find it easier to lend their presence rather than donate hard cash.

Just as Donald Trump proclaimed he could shoot someone in the middle of Fifth Avenue and not lose any votes, the antics and extravagance of royal families seem remarkably untroubling to their subjects. Several television shows — *The Royals* and *The Windsors* — rely on almost defamatory satires of the British royal family, who have been tarnished by scandals surrounding Princes Andrew and Harry. But the most improper behaviour by royalty rarely leads to the monarchy itself being seriously questioned. It's not as if these went unnoticed: there is a small library chronicling the quite remarkable behaviour of the extended Windsor clan.[13]

There are limits, as Juan Carlos of Spain discovered when a series of family scandals led to his abdication in 2014, but clearly this is a very different world from the one in which Edward VIII was forced to abdicate. The most extreme case came in 2001 when the crown prince of Nepal killed ten members of his family and died himself. A few years after the massacre, the unpopular King Gyanendra, having suspended the constitution, was deposed, and a republic declared. There are occasional calls for his restoration from right-wing Hindu politicians, and Gyanendra remains in Nepal, perhaps hoping one day for his restoration.

# Institutions matter

How we organise political systems and how they achieve legitimacy are not always fashionable questions, but they are central to creating and maintaining a democratic polity. Balancing the need for an effective and accountable state while preserving individual freedom is central to any democratic constitution. In her discussion of constitutionalism, Hannah Arendt quotes Montesquieu's insight that 'even virtue stands in need of limitation'.[1]

There are many countries in which the president is head of state without being head of the executive government, and there are a range of ways in which such heads are chosen. Monarchists argue that presidents do not have the same legitimacy as a hereditary ruler, although Germany has managed major political transformations over the past half-century, including the reunification of the country, with several appointed and largely non-partisan presidents. Defenders of monarchy claim that it promotes national unity in ways that no elected head of state can, because of the myth that the monarch is above politics and able to represent the entire nation. In one of the more articulate defences of the system, Akilesh Pillalamarri argued that had Afghanistan restored its monarch after the Taliban was overthrown in 2001, it might have saved the country some of the subsequent unrest.[2]

For true believers, royalty is 'an institution that occupies a place in the heart of the ordinary citizen, while remaining above and beyond the turmoil of politics, a court of appeal to that every faction, every ethnic group and every religious confession may address itself'. The English conservative Roger Scruton wrote this in the lead-up to the breakup of Czechoslovakia, suggesting — presumably seriously — that a solution to problems in Slovakia was to again crown an emperor of Hungary in Bratislava.[3]

All democratic systems need a balance between executive and legislative power, and some means of adjudicating between them when conflicts arise. The range of liberal-democratic structures is considerable, from elected presidents who head the executive branch, as in the United States and most of Latin America, through to largely ceremonial heads of state, with executive powers vested in the legislature. Some countries, such as France and Poland, have hybrid models, where power is shared between the president and the parliament, both directly elected; the United States has an elaborate system of checks and balances, which give both Congress and the president extensive veto powers over the other. Attempts to measure the strength of democracy, such as *The Economist*'s 'Democracy Index', score parliamentary systems, whether headed by monarchs or presidents, better than those where executive power rests with the president.

There are many examples of parliamentary systems in which the presidency is largely ceremonial and effectively under the control of the elected government. Ireland has a parliamentary government with an elected president, and India, Italy, and Germany have electoral colleges, combining national and regional legislators. In these systems even a popularly elected president must take the advice of the executive, as in the case of Austria when a Green president swore in a right-wing government in 2017. But at moments of political crisis even a figurehead president will have political authority, especially if there is no clear parliamentary majority. The Israeli president plays an active role in negotiations to form a government where there is no conclusive parliamentary majority; in Portugal, President Sampaio intervened to limit Portuguese participation in the Iraq War. Successive Italian presidents have been more actively involved in political decisions than the constitutional monarchs of Western Europe, and German presidents have deferred legislation on grounds of possible constitutional impropriety.

The classic definition of constitutional monarchy is based on Walter Bagehot's book *The English Constitution* (1867), in which he summed up the role of the sovereign as providing a 'disguise' for the real workings of government, retaining only 'the right to be consulted, the right to encourage, the right to warn'. Bagehot was an unabashed elitist who feared the possibility of universal suffrage, but his distinction between the 'dignified' and the 'efficient' parts of government has become the basis of all constitutional monarchies since. He was also editor of *The Economist* for seventeen years, which might explain that publication's exasperation with the continuing grip of royalty on the British imagination.

A constitutional monarch is bound to follow the advice of the elected government; but except in countries such as Sweden and Japan, where the monarch is explicitly excluded from acting, it is not always clear how much leeway the monarch has if there is no clear parliamentary majority, or where a government appears to act in breach of the constitution. Britain is unique in that it has no written constitution, leaving open the possibility of a monarch intervening when there is no clear parliamentary majority.

Constitutional monarchs reign, but they do not rule, although they may exert power behind the scenes. In one of the few political-science articles that looks at monarchies comparatively, the authors make an important distinction between 'constitutional' and 'democratic parliamentary' monarchies, the latter being ones where it is clear that the monarch has no political prerogatives, although the sovereign may still exercise indirect influence based on status and access.[4] Discovering the extent of such indirect influence is extremely difficult, as there appears to be a code that prevents government leaders ever frankly acknowledging the substance of their discussion with monarchs. It is unlikely that prime ministers do not at times seek to frame their advice in ways that they believe will win the approval of the sovereign, and there are several indications of this in accounts of ministerial meetings with Queen Elizabeth. One assumes other constitutional monarchs adopt the Queen's tactics of indicating disapproval 'by a significant failure to comment'.[5]

Parliamentary governments, whether monarchical or not, clearly differ from the presidential systems of the United States and much of Latin America. The pomp and ceremony attributed to the US president — Air Force One; 'Hail to the Chief', etcetera — is far greater than that possessed by a head of government who is also not head of state. The American yearning for the panoply of monarchy was evident in the references to John F Kennedy's rule as a new Camelot, but even modest presidents such as Jimmy Carter are surrounded by fanfare. It is, of course, the case, as Anthony Sampson argued in the case of Tony Blair, that contemporary prime ministers increasingly claim the trappings of state,[6] but it is more difficult for a leader who in theory is responsible to an apolitical head of state to argue that he represents that national will. Indeed, a United States federal judge had occasion to remind Trump that he was not a king after Trump claimed unlimited executive power to prevent testimony from former officials to his first impeachment hearing in November 2019.[7] As Chief Justice

Roberts wrote, quoting the first American chief justice: 'A king is born to power and can do no wrong. The President, by contrast, is "of the people" and subject to the law.' Most monarchs have retained sovereign immunity; this was last tested in Britain in 1911, when a judge ruled that George V could not be required to give evidence in a bigamy case.

In general, parliamentary systems with a presidential head of state follow Bagehot's distinction between the dignified and efficient functions of government. The President of India, for example, 'represents the Nation but does not rule the Nation. He is the symbol of the Nation. His place in the administration is that of a ceremonial device on a seal by that the nation's decisions are made known.'[8] The crucial difference is that the President of India is chosen by legislators, thus giving a dominant political party the opportunity to install someone who is not seen as standing above politics. Whether a president is popularly elected or chosen by the legislature, she will inevitably come with a political persona that a clever royal heir can avoid.

Anyone who is elected president, however eminent, will have a political history that is open to scrutiny. Even the leftist political historian Eric Hobsbawm defended constitutional monarchy, because it avoided the difficulty of choosing a head of state.[9] But Ireland's experience suggests that a popularly elected president can effectively both represent the country and provide a check on the government. Mary Robinson, who was that country's president from 1990 to 1997, and a former Labour politician, was generally regarded as giving the position genuine significance and became enormously popular, despite a bitter election campaign in which she was not the clear front-runner. Robinson showed it is possible to transcend party allegiances to become a symbol of national unity; however, there are only a few other small countries, such as Austria, Iceland, and Slovenia, in which a popularly elected president has no executive function.

No one set of arrangements is by itself capable of resisting the rise of authoritarian and anti-democratic governments that then set about changing the rules which brought them to power. This was the trajectory of fascism in inter-war Europe, and it is being repeated today in countries such as Turkey, Poland, and Venezuela. It is generally assumed that the division of powers provides some protection for democracy, although this is no more than repeating the old adage that power corrupts, and that absolute power corrupts absolutely. But in an era when the Prime Minister of Hungary can boast of support for 'illiberal democracy', meaning majority rule with no respect for minorities or freedom of expression, re-examining the basic institutions seems important.

Even where they are restricted constitutionally, monarchs may exercise considerable hidden influence on the political culture of their realm. As Philip Murphy wrote, reflecting on the impact of Elizabeth II, 'An extremely long-reigning monarch can shape the political landscape like an iceberg; by steadily maintaining the same course, they can exert a powerful influence on our collective values.'[10] Even the most symbolic monarchy can intervene subtly in national conversations, as was demonstrated by Emperor Akihito in his reaching out to victims of Japanese aggression, and by the decision of Crown Prince Naruhito to speak at the International AIDS Conference in Yokohama in 1994, appearing on stage with an openly positive Japanese man. I was at that conference, and I recall seeing his speech appearing across every television network that evening.

In Western democracies, monarchies have survived by yielding political power in return for wealth and social status. Apparent wealth can be misleading; the poorest royal family in Europe, the Norwegians, get by with access to several palaces, a yacht, and a royal train, but they could hardly dispose of these for private gain. Equally, the Emperor of Japan resides in a palace that occupies vast grounds in the centre of Tokyo, but he could not decide to develop the grounds into condominiums, and he lives far less lavishly than most other royals. Northern European royals like to present themselves as living simply — the Dutch queen doing her shopping; the Swedish king driving himself to work — but too often this appearance disguises considerable extravagance. There was an outcry in the Netherlands when it emerged that the ruling family had spent two million euros for a luxury yacht during the height of the coronavirus pandemic.

If there is confusion between the private wealth of the

sovereign and their access to state resources, almost every royal family depends upon subventions from the state, often a cause of bitter dispute. One recent estimate for Western Europe suggests that the British family costs tax-payers £82 million a year, while the Spanish and Swedes get by on less than one-tenth of that amount. On a per capita basis, however, the most expensive royal family seems to be the Norwegian, at £34 million.[11] It's worth noting that even a relatively low-key ceremonial German presidency is estimated to cost more than most European monarchies.

Beyond any formal involvement, the wealth and access of royal families means they are inexorably entwined with power elites. That access is both national and global; members of royal families often attend events such as the World Economic Forum in Davos, where in 2020 Prince Charles gave a keynote address on the environment, following a number of expressions of royal interest in tackling climate change. Prince Bernhard of the Netherlands was the initial chair of the Bilderberg Meeting, an informal gathering of political and business leaders from Western Europe and the United States, which has been attended by members of five ruling families. (Bernhard was forced to stand down after allegations of bribery by the Lockheed Corporation.) Unlike Davos, Bilderberg meetings are largely secret, but they allow for informal connections between ostensibly apolitical sovereigns and the controllers of political and economic power. The abuse of royal connections for personal enrichment has been most obvious in the case of Spain's Juan Carlos and Britain's Prince Andrew, but it is hardly limited to them. Protesters in Jordan during the Arab Spring referred to King Abdullah and his entourage as 'Ali Baba and the forty thieves', and the greed of the Thai king was a central grievance of the student protests of 2020.

While intermarriage between royal families has declined, there remains a certain solidarity, which allows governments to foster links, sometimes opaque, as in the case of relations between the British and the Saudi royal families. British schools and military academies still attract a range of royal students; the current King of Malaysia, Sultan Abdullah, and the Crown Prince of Abu Dhabi studied together at the Royal Military Academy at Sandhurst, which lists royalty from twenty-three countries among its graduates. The current Japanese emperor studied at Oxford, which awarded him an honorary doctorate. When Queen Elizabeth celebrated her diamond jubilee in 2012, nineteen ruling monarchs were pictured in a ceremonial photo with the Queen, along with four pretenders to deposed European thrones. An equal gathering of royals had joined celebrations for King Bhumipol's sixtieth year on the Thai throne six years earlier.

However limited their formal powers, the influence of constitutional monarchs is largely exerted in private and is unaccountable to any democratic process. Almost a century ago, George Bernard Shaw's play *The Apple Cart* posited a monarch who threatens to resign and run for popular election. Although a socialist, Shaw's sympathies were surprisingly monarchical, and in a long monologue King Magnus gives a stirring defence of his position. The play was first produced in 1928 — oddly, in Warsaw — but in a preface written several years later, Shaw repeats extravagant claims for the monarch:

> George III and Queen Victoria were not, like Queen Elizabeth, the natural superiors of their ministers in political genius and general capacity; but they were for many purposes of state necessarily superior to them in experience, in cunning, and in exact knowledge of the limits of their responsibility and consequently of the limits of their irresponsibility — in short, in the authority and practical power that these superiorities produce.[12]

The same theme appeared in the book and television series *To Play the King*, and Mike Bartlett's play *Charles III* takes up this theme in the contemporary world. Indeed, former royalty play a major role in electoral politics in several countries. After the fall of communism in Bulgaria, the former King Simeon II returned and served as prime minister from 2001 to 2005; the ruling BJP has appointed a number of erstwhile royals, including the titular king of Manipur, to the Indian upper house; while the heir to the Austro-Hungarian throne, Otto von Habsburg, sat in the European Parliament for twenty years and was a genuine force for European integration. In 2019 King

Vajiralongkorn of Thailand forbade his sister, Princess Ubolratana Mahidol, from running for office, although she had renounced her royal titles after marrying an American in the 1970s. She was allied with exiled prime minister Thaksin Shinawatra, and her candidacy would have been a remarkable affront to the monarch. However, no royal figure has matched the career of Norodom Sihanouk, who was twice king of Cambodia, and prime minister for fifteen years, before the triumph of the Khmer Rouge.

# Royal fluffery: do we really need a Princess Michael of Kent?

The British royals are undoubtedly the best-known and most reported-on family in the world. Queen Elizabeth has now reigned for longer than any previous British monarch; as I write, planning is underway to mark her seventieth year on the throne in 2022 — that is, a platinum anniversary. When she dies there will inevitably be questions about the continued relevance of the monarchy, despite the Windsor line now being assured for another three generations. It is unlikely that this will promote a serious discussion of republicanism, except perhaps in the Antipodes, where the persistence of a very British monarch as head of state of remains a constant irritant to many . When he was Labour leader, Jeremy Corbyn had to deny claims that he would seek to abolish the monarchy, which even the party's left accepted would be deeply unpopular. While running to succeed Corbyn as Labour leader, Clive Lewis called for a referendum on abolishing the monarchy, but his campaign failed to win the support of sufficient MPs to proceed. The successful candidate, Sir Keir Starmer, boasts of his investiture at Buckingham Palace. Meanwhile, the remaining countries that retain the British monarch as head of state — including small-island Caribbean and Pacific states — seem largely uninterested, or lack the political will, to change the status quo.

Indeed, there was deeper republican sentiment in nineteenth-century Britain than there seems to be today. In the 1870s the National Republican League was formed; in the 1920s the British Labour Party debated abolishing the monarchy. Yet, writing thirty years ago, the historian David Cannadine suggested, 'If, as seems possible, the next coronation takes place without a house of lords, a Commonwealth or an Established Church, the role of the ceremonial in creating the comforting picture of stability, tradition and continuity will only be further enhanced.'[1] Henry James's description of his reaction to the death of Queen Victoria might well stand as an obituary for the present Queen: 'the safe and motherly old middle-class Queen, who held the nation warm under the fold of her big, hideous Scotch-plaid shawl.' Victoria, comments Julia Baird, 'had become a kind of talisman and decorum, a shield against upsetting turmoil'.[2]

In one sense, Britain is not a constitutional monarchy, for it has no written constitution, and all government is conducted as if it were at the pleasure of the monarch.

Britons remain defined as subjects rather than citizens; Norman Baker points to the paradox that were members of parliament elected on a pledge to abolish the monarchy, they would first need to promise allegiance to her when sworn in.[3] (Equally, the Queen would presumably need to sign a parliamentary bill to remove herself from office.) Unlike Britain, the Commonwealth countries that have retained the monarchy have written constitutions, which in most cases recognise the reserve powers of the Crown, which in Britain remain uncodified. Through meetings of the Privy Council, which the Queen attends but is essentially the preserve of the government, regulations and appointments are made without the bother of passing through parliament, an example of how the mystique of monarchy acts to obfuscate the power of the state. The Privy Council remains the final court of appeal for some small Commonwealth nations.

During her reign of almost seventy years, Elizabeth has met regularly with a total of fourteen prime ministers, some of them not born when she came to the throne. It is extraordinary how little we know of how she has exercised her right to 'be consulted, to encourage and to warn', though this did not prevent Peter Morgan from imagining royal conversations in both his play *The Audience* and the very successful TV series *The Crown*. In the latter, Morgan depicts the Queen lecturing her first prime minister, Winston Churchill, on the lessons she had learnt from studying Bagehot, and expressing doubts about the Suez adventure to Sir Anthony Eden. But we should beware of seeing *The Crown* as other than fiction, with its own biases, as shown in the airbrushing of the Duke of Windsor's long flirtation with Nazi Germany and the crude misportrayal of Australian prime minister Bob Hawke.

Morgan suggested that the Queen had a particularly warm relationship with Labour prime minister Harold Wilson, and a frostier one with the Tory prime minister Margaret Thatcher. Their views were most divergent around the role of the Commonwealth — about which more later. For a Conservative prime minister, Thatcher seemed surprisingly uninterested in royal approval; possibly, they both felt slightly uncomfortable in the unusual situation of women heading both the 'dignified' and 'efficient' business of government. Thatcher may well have shared some of the left's contempt for the sense of entitlement that marks so much of the royal family's behaviour. It is hard not to feel some sympathy with the fictional Thatcher in the excruciating episode of *The Crown* where she struggles to adjust to royal eccentricities while a guest at Balmoral. Reports suggest that the Queen had a warmer relationship with Theresa May during May's unhappy three years as prime minister.

More recent prime ministers have become slightly less discreet: Tony Blair is said to have remarked that 'the Queen was the only person with whom he could expatiate on the fine personal qualities of his colleagues'.[4] David Cameron had to apologise to the Queen after he revealed to former

New York mayor Michael Bloomberg that she had 'purred down the line' when he informed her that Scotland had voted against independence, and Boris Johnson reported that when he went to the Palace to be sworn in, the Queen told him, 'I don't know why anyone would want the job.'

There have been moments during Elizabeth's long reign when she has been called on to use her reserve powers, most notably when two Conservative prime ministers — Sir Anthony Eden in 1957 and Harold Macmillan in 1963 — resigned. In both cases, the Conservative Party retained a clear majority in the House of Commons but had no clear process to choose a replacement leader, and the Queen sought advice from several party elders. Particularly in the latter case, when Macmillan strongly advised the Queen to appoint Lord Douglas-Home, there were other seemingly stronger candidates. In his study of the Queen, Ben Pimlott concludes that her choice of Douglas-Home was 'the biggest political misjudgement of her reign'.[5] Since then, the Conservative Party has established rules to appoint their leader, but the reserve powers of the monarch to appoint and dismiss a prime minister were crucial in the 1975 constitutional crisis in Australia.

It seems that the Queen has essentially followed Bagehot's advice to pursue 'well considered inaction' — not always the case with her son and heir, Prince Charles, who has publicly expressed his views on a range of issues, and has privately lobbied government ministers. (Some of his letters to government ministers, termed the black spider memos, were released after an order of the Supreme Court in 2015.) As William Gilbert said of the House of Lords, they do nothing in particular, but they do it very well. But even if the Queen does no more than nod and keep the conversation flowing, it is inconceivable that ministers are not conscious of her reactions. Whether they are swayed by these reactions is less clear.

Nor do there seem to be many expectations that the monarch should intervene. Allegations that Prime Minister Johnson misled the Queen over the proroguing of parliament in 2019 did not in the end cost Johnson politically, despite a ruling by the Supreme Court that his suspension of parliamentary sittings was unlawful. Johnson had sought to prorogue sittings of the House of Commons to avoid the possible defeat of his Brexit plans, a move that required approval by the Privy Council. There were suggestions at the time that the Queen could have refused to agree, but it seems unlikely that she would not have taken the advice of the prime minister, whatever personal reservations she may have felt.

The real political significance of the British royals is their perpetuation of a deeply entrenched class system, symbolised by the retention of some hereditary peers in the House of Lords — a feudal remnant that has no counterpart elsewhere in Europe. (The Lords, which numbers many hundreds of members, mainly appointed by successive governments, also include ninety hereditary peers chosen from among themselves, plus twenty-six bishops of the Church of England.) The Queen may have abolished 'coming out' balls, admitted television cameras into the royal residences, and invited a cross-section of British society to Buckingham Palace garden parties, but the royals are a constant reminder of the importance of family background, accent, and the right school. There is a strong argument that the monarchy serves to legitimise the continuing reality of class relations and essentially to provide camouflage for persisting inequality and elitist rule. Class barriers persist in Britain, as evidenced by the two-thirds of Boris Johnson's cabinet who come from private schools that educate 7 per cent of the population. Among significant OECD countries, only the United States has a more unequal distribution of wealth than Britain.

A forthcoming book by Laura Clancy, *Staging the Royal Family: the cultural politics of the British monarchy*, makes this argument persuasively. Conceptualising the monarchy as a firm — the term first adopted by George VI — she argues that we cannot divorce the current family from 'the processes of capital accumulation, profit extraction and other forms of exploitation' that have created the complex web of financial holdings presided over by the Queen and the Prince of Wales.[6] As she points out, the Crown makes its wealth visible through its public performances, while 'the sources, mechanisms and processes of wealth are rendered invisible and inscrutable'. Much of this wealth comes from the Crown Estate, a collection of lands and other holdings that functions as the sovereign's personal estate and is technically neither the property of the British government nor that of the royal family. Including 263,000 farmed acres, a significant portion of the buildings in central London, and about half of the UK shoreline, including twelve miles of seabed extending out beyond those coasts, the Crown Estate's holdings in 2019 were calculated to have a capital value of £14.3 billion. This is justified, as *The Economist*, hardly a left-wing publication, put it, by 'the Royals injecting pageantry, romance, mystery and drama into the lives of British people, mitigating the dreary business of being a cog in the wheels of capitalism'.[7]

Clancy joins a long list of authors chronicling the abuses of the British royal family, such as Joan Smith's 2015 'provocation', *Down With the Royals*. The most recent example comes from former Liberal Democrat minister Norman Baker. In his book *And What Do YOU Do?*, he provides a coruscating analysis of the financial rorts and wasteful use of public funds by the extended royal family that suggests at least several of them are guilty of criminal behaviour in their misuse of public funds and access to government. The casual use of helicopters and the royal train when there are adequate public alternatives available is particularly striking, as is Prince Charles's combination of profligate spending on himself and his shrewdness in billing private expenses to the public purse. The historian Robert Lacey has claimed that '[m]aking too much money is considered taboo',[8] but few members of the current family seem to have heeded his advice.

At the beginning of 2021 *The Guardian* disclosed the extent to which an opaque device known as 'the Queen's consent' allows the royal family to have input into any proposed legislation that might be regarded as impacting on 'the prerogative or interests of the crown'. These interests appear to have been very broadly interpreted, allowing the Queen to review laws affecting rail developments, housing, animal welfare, and, unsurprisingly, measures concerning trusts and taxation. It appears the palace has been assiduous in protecting the secrecy that surrounds the wealth and financial obligations of the Windsor family.[9]

A study by Brand Finance in 2017 estimated that the monarchy generated £1.76 billion for the UK economy and cost the British taxpayers £292 million.[10] Were it a business, the report concluded, it would be the third-biggest brand in the world. Their conclusion is based upon a number of generous assumptions about the returns from royal involvement; after all, a British republic could still trade off nostalgia for its imperial past, as any number of historical dramas illustrate. It does not require a living monarch to draw tourists to palaces such as Versailles or St Petersburg's Winter Palace. A vast range of royal memorabilia marks every royal wedding or birth; one might celebrate the wedding of the Queen's grand-daughter, Princess Beatrice, ninth in line to the throne, with 'a china tankard and pillbox, shortbread biscuits, strawberry truffles and a tea towel, with all items featuring the image of a bee — a play on Beatrice's name to family and friends'. On the other hand, the report doesn't estimate the increased circulation of newspapers and magazines when there is a new royal scandal.

Royal patronage is much sought after, and the extended family are kept busy supporting charities across the country. In the website created by the Duke and Duchess of Sussex — that is, Harry and Meghan — after they first left royal duties, they proclaim that 'Her Majesty serves as a symbol of unity and national pride', and follow this with a long list of the organisations that benefit from royal patronage and their own causes, ranging from rhino preservation to rugby football. By withdrawing from royal duties they have exchanged these patronages for the benefits of major commercial sponsorships.

The royals work assiduously; the Princess Royal — Harry's aunt Anne — is patron of over 300 organisations, and chancellor of five universities, presumably not too onerous a task. Yet the independent think tank Giving Evidence found that having a prince or duchess as patron has no clear financial benefit, while 74 per cent of charities under royal patronage had received no visit from their patron in the previous year.[11]

What matters for the survival of monarchy is that its members are seen to be busy, well groomed in the latest, preferably British, fashion, and ready to smile through yet another tedious stone-laying or charity evening. When he was Prince of Wales, the future Edward VIII referred to a life divided between 'furious bouts of "princing" — opening hospitals, addressing dinners, receiving addresses, smiling, smiling, smiling — and tracts of emptiness that it was up to him to fill as best he could'.[12] In some cases, such as Princess Diana's public support for people with AIDS, or Princess Anne's work with Save the Children, members of the royal family do more than just lend their name. In other examples, such as Prince Philip's fondness for big-game hunting while a leading member of the World Wildlife Fund, one can only admire royal hypocrisy. And the royals travel constantly; the Queen herself has visited every Commonwealth nation but Rwanda and Cameroon, both of which are recent additions. These visits are carefully designed to project Britain's place in the world, sometimes to favour the hosts, as in the case of her first royal tour, along with her parents, to South Africa in 1947, which prime minister Jan Smuts hoped might help maintain his government in power. His party was, however, defeated by the pro-apartheid Nationals the following year. Younger members of 'the firm' are regularly dispatched overseas — sometimes, one suspects, to dampen republican sentiment in the remaining dominions.

Among the European monarchies, the British royal family stands out for its sheer size, encompassing four generations and surviving cousins of the Queen, such as the Dukes of Kent and Gloucester. (For anyone who cares, Princess Michael is the wife of one of the Queen's cousins; were some mysterious plague to eliminate forty-eight members of the royal family, her husband would inherit the throne.) In Scandinavia and Spain, on the other hand, the royal family is defined more narrowly, consisting of the present king, the queen consort, their children, and his parents. Not all members of the British royal family are supported directly by the state, although there are clearly associated costs of security and transport when anyone with royal trappings turns up to open an event. In 2010 Scotland Yard acknowledged it provided security for twenty-two royals, an excessive figure by any but Saudi standards. Members of the extended family live in the world's most exclusive boarding house, Kensington Palace, which doubles as a tourist attraction.

And despite continuing claims of reducing expenditure, the royal households include large numbers of retainers, whose titles are medieval even if their contemporary roles remain obscure: should one wonder what functions are performed by the Gold and Silver Sticks-in-Waiting, it is reassuring to know that these are not full-time positions. No other European monarchy is so wedded to traditional displays of pomp; it is unlikely that when Charles is crowned he will be content with simply taking an oath in front of the parliament buildings, which is how Felipe was sworn in as King of Spain.

Common to much of the British debate on monarchy is the view that monarchies survive because they provide a constant source of romantic escapism. (Dreams of royalty are frequently reported.) There is a whole sub-genre of novels that imagine British royalty in various situations; Elizabeth George, the American Anglophile mystery writer, begins one of her books with a milkman fantasising a conversation with the Queen. In the Netflix television series *Sex Education*, one boy asks, 'Is it weird that I always think about the Queen when I come?' There are more disturbing stories of obsessive preoccupation with royalty; Queen Victoria was subject to eight attempts on her life, and several attempts have been made on the current royal family, including the successful assassination of the Queen's second cousin, Lord Louis Mountbatten, in 1979. (Mountbatten had been Admiral of the Fleet and the last viceroy in India, and was a father figure for both Princes Philip and Charles.)

Despite a series of scandals and marriage break-ups, the popularity of the British royals has increased as respect for politicians has declined; when the Queen gave a short, anodyne address during the 2020 COVID-19 pandemic, it was hailed as if it were a great act of states(wo)manship. I suspect that most Britons are aware of the excesses of royal privilege, and enjoy the royals as a continuing soap opera, a family drama in which everyone can partake. The combination of symbolic power and family dysfunction makes for continuing entertainment that a presidential system cannot provide. At the same time, they preserve the illusion of Britain as a great power, propped up by elaborate ceremony that claims far greater historical continuity than is, in fact, the case — what Tom Nairn characterised as 'the glamour of backwardness'.[13] As one observer wrote:

Sometimes, as when I watched the 12-year-old Prince Harry walk behind the coffin of his mother, Princess Diana, I think monarchy is less a national enchantment, or hoax, than a national sickness. I have done a jigsaw puzzle of the queen's face. I bought it at the gift shop at Sandringham, the queen's country home. What is that but an act of control by the subject of the object? ... The royal family is a sacrifice at the centre of Britain's national life, fuel for the creation of a national soul because we can't think of anything better.[14]

This sense of grudging sympathy for the royal family seems fairly widespread. As Hilary Mantel, whose Wolf Hall trilogy on Thomas Cromwell's role in the reign of Henry VIII won her two Booker prizes, confessed:

I used to think that the interesting issue was whether we should have a monarchy or not. But now I think that question is rather like, should we have pandas or not? Our current royal family doesn't have the difficulties in breeding that pandas do, but pandas and royal persons alike are expensive to conserve and ill-adapted to any modern environment ... It may be that the whole phenomenon of monarchy is irrational, but that doesn't mean that when we look at it we should behave like spectators at Bedlam.[15]

Monarchs provide a continuing symbol of national identity that is constantly reinvented. The image of the

British sovereign has appeared on every British postage stamp since the invention of the 'Penny Black' in 1840; indeed, one clear example of the Queen's involvement in politics came during the Labour government of Harold Wilson, when she effectively vetoed postmaster-general Tony Benn's attempt to remove her image. Her profile is sufficient to identify the stamp as coming from the United Kingdom. No one has appeared on stamps more than Queen Elizabeth, but the ubiquity of the British royals is shown on stamps commemorating Princes Diana from countries as unlikely as Paraguay, Benin, and even North Korea, presumably for sale to overseas collectors. (Most monarchies depict their sovereigns on stamps and banknotes, although Japan largely eschews this.) Along with Japan and Tonga, Britain is one of the few countries whose national anthem honours the sovereign.

The British royals are part of the constant packaging of nostalgia as a successful export industry, symbolised by the enormous success of the television series *Downton Abbey,* now a film that extols the importance of monarchy. The royals exert an unmatched hold over the global imagination, not least because of continuing American fascination with them. Perhaps the foremost academic expert on the British monarchy, Frank Prochaska, has claimed that 'Americans fell under the spell of royal tradition from the lofty heights of republican virtue'.[16] British governments have used this enchantment to pursue the illusion of the 'special relation-ship' between the two countries, as in the royal visit paid by George VI and Queen Elizabeth to the United States in 1939, deliberately aimed at building American support for the likely forthcoming war with Germany. Most recently, President Trump was accorded a full state visit in 2019, which produced excruciating pictures of Trump towering over the Queen as he brought his full adult family along to meet her.

Just as Sarah Ferguson, the estranged wife of Prince Andrew, appeared on American television, including Donald Trump's *Celebrity Apprentice*, the decision of Prince Harry and Meghan Markle to move to California, and the extensive interview with Oprah, was a tacit recognition of the inexhaustible American appetite for royal gossip. Whether the couple can surmount the sense of irrelevancy that was the fate of Harry's great-great-uncle, the Duke of Windsor, remains to be seen. The celebrity status of Princess Diana only increased after her divorce and the removal of her status as a 'royal highness'.

The potent mixture of celebrity and tradition are powerful forces supporting the persistence of monarchy. Nearly thirty years ago, Christopher Hitchens wrote a counterblast against the British monarchy. He ended his pamphlet by asking the British people to reflect on abolishing royalty: 'Do you prefer invented tradition, sanitised history, prettified literature, state-sponsored superstition and media-dominated pulses of cheering and jeering?'[17] The royal family has weathered a number of storms since Hitchens wrote; certainly, the perception of insensitivity to the death of Diana and the subsequent marriage of Charles and Camilla seemed to suggest what the writer Bea Campbell called a 'sub-republican rumbling in the discontent'.[18] But two decades and several scandals later, the royals seem to have retained popular support. After the Golden Jubilee of the Queen, and the frenzy surrounding the next generation of royal princes and their wives, it appears that most people in Britain are satisfied with the status quo.

It is possible that the accession of Charles as king will reopen a republican debate. Back in 2004, Anthony Sampson wrote, 'The future of the monarchy, and of the eccentric heir apparent, now seems more uncertain than at any time in the last century.'[19] *The Economist* more recently described Charles as having a 'new ageism meets neo-feudalism' view of the world,[20] and there are widely known stories about his meanness, petulance, and vanity.[21] My hunch is that when the Queen dies, the desire for continuity will produce a surge of affection for her heir.

# The dominions

The British monarchy is unique in that it provides the head of state for fifteen other countries, which have what could be called a Gilbertian political system: the head of state is rarely present, and is represented by a governor-general, who is often a senior jurist or military officer, or, in Canada's case, a distinguished journalist. Some supporters of an independent Scotland have suggested that they would no longer retain the British monarch, although the present royal family are heirs to the last separate Scottish monarchy. In most cases, the governor-general is appointed by the prime minister, although Papua New Guinea requires a vote of the national parliament. Originally, governors-general were members of the British aristocracy, including several royal princes, but this practice has been largely abandoned. The Australian Labor government upset George V when it insisted on appointing an Australian, Sir Isaac Isaacs, to the position in 1931, but it was not until 1952 that Canada appointed a local, with New Zealand following in 1967. Canadian and New Zealand prime ministers have been more concerned than Australia to reflect diversity in their choices.

There have been some high-profile governors-general — notably in Canada and New Zealand — but it was striking that when major bushfires raged across Australia at the end of 2019 there was an outcry at the absence of the prime minister, then holidaying in Hawaii. That the governor-general was also abroad — visiting troops — went largely unnoticed. In Australia and Canada, each state or province also has an appointed head of state representing the monarch. The relationship of the Queen to her governors-general is somewhat opaque; they are each appointed by her, but on the advice of the national government. They are not subject to the direction, supervision, or veto of the monarch, although the Australian governor-general Sir John Kerr relied on advice from the Palace in the constitutional crisis of 1975 (of which more later). That prime ministers often have sole discretion in choosing the head of state to whom they are nominally accountable removes the major political guarantee that monarchists claim for the system. If governors-general are to have any powers at all, it is inappropriate that they are the personal gifts bestowed by a prime minister.

The Statute of Westminster in 1931 recognised six countries as independent of Britain but subject to the Crown: Ireland and South Africa have now abandoned the monarchy, while Newfoundland became part of Canada. Of the remaining 'old Dominions', public opinion polls in

Canada, New Zealand, and Australia show fluctuating sup-port for the monarchy but little real concern with the status quo. Large numbers of people are theoretically republican, but, like the Queen in *Alice Through the Looking Glass*, want 'jam to-morrow and jam yesterday — but never jam to-day'. An all-white constituency in South Africa voted to become a republic in 1960, while Australia rejected a republican model in 1999. The very small island nations of Tuvalu and Saint Vincent and the Grenadines have also rejected repub-licanism in referenda. The government of Barbados declared its intention to become a republic in 2021, leading some British Tories to claim this was due to Chinese pressure.

Canada appears the most committed to retaining the royal connection, although clearly Quebec nationalists would dispense with a British queen as part of secession. For English-speaking Canadians, one suspects the royals are important as another reminder that they are not part of the United States. Considerable efforts have been made to frame the monarchy as essentially Canadian, defining 'the Crown' as a crucial part of the Canadian constitution: 'The Canadian innovation has been to keep monarchy, while turning a non-resident monarch into less of a physical presence and more of an abstraction.'[1] D. Michael Jackson, president of the Institute for the Study of the Crown, argues that the Crown 'penetrates, permeates, colours and enables all aspects of the Canadian constitutional arrangements', including relations with indigenous peoples. The Ontario Court of Appeal has made clear that swearing allegiance to the Queen of Canada

is 'swearing allegiance to a symbol of our form of government
... It is not an oath to a foreign sovereign.'[2] Nonetheless,
immediately after Prince Harry's announcement that he was
withdrawing from royal duties there was popular support in
Canada for the idea of naming him governor-general.

In most countries the monarchy remains as a symbol of
national identity, but in those Commonwealth countries
that retain the British sovereign as head of state it works
to perpetuate colonial ties that affront republicans. Getting
rid of the monarchy is not as much about changing the
arrangements of government as it is about a symbolic
break with past British influence. Ireland formally became
a republic in 1949, two years after India, and most of
Britain's former colonies followed, led by Ghana in 1957
and Tanganyika in 1961. (Pakistan and Sri Lanka took
somewhat longer.) Perhaps surprisingly, this has not been
the pattern for former colonies in the Caribbean, despite
the expression of republican sentiments, especially in
Jamaica, where both major parties favour the change but
have yet to organise the required referendum. In Grenada
the monarchy even survived a Marxist coup in 1979;
indeed, then governor-general Paul Scoon secretly signalled that he supported the American military invasion
of 1983 — without, it appears, informing the Palace. After
the invasion, Scoon became interim head of government
and appointed an advisory council, which governed until
post-invasion elections the following year. Scoon remained
as governor-general for seven more years.

# Getting rid of the Queen: the failed Australian republican movement

Republicanism in Australia dates back to the radical movements of the 1890s, but rarely gained much popular support until the 1990s. The role of the Queen came under considerable scrutiny when, in 1975, the governor-general, Sir John Kerr, dismissed the Whitlam government on the grounds that the Senate was refusing to vote on bills required for continuing government expenditure. After considerable efforts to prevent access to letters between Kerr and the Palace, a High Court decision in favour of historian Jenny Hocking led to the release of this correspondence in July 2020, which showed that Kerr had relied heavily on advice from the Palace supporting his use of the reserve powers of the Crown to dismiss a properly constituted government. Debate as to whether this implied direct influence on Australian politics from the Crown continues; the constitutional lawyer Anne Twomey concluded 'The letters, instead of showing the Palace interfered in the dismissal of Whitlam, showed that Whitlam sought Palace interference but didn't get it. We are an independent country after all.'[1]

However, I am persuaded by Hocking's argument that the advice from the Palace raised no objections to a use of 'reserve powers' that went beyond anything the Queen herself has relied upon in Britain.[2] Both Kerr and his wife were subsequently rewarded with royal honours, and subsequently Prince Charles expressed support for Kerr's actions and may have been angling — unsuccessfully — to be appointed governor-general himself. Given the very hostile reactions to Kerr's actions, the use of the reserve powers by a future governor-general seems highly unlikely.

Whitlam's dismissal focused attention on the Australian constitution, and the foundation of the Australian Republican Movement in 1990 put the issue on the mainstream agenda. In 1995 prime minister Paul Keating met with the Queen to inform her that he would argue for an Australian republic. In his account of that meeting, he wrote that he was struck by 'the continuing fantasy she was forced to play out'.[3] Keating was replaced in 1996 by a conservative government led by John Howard, who agreed to a referendum while personally opposing the change. In 1999 Australians rejected a proposal to establish a republic, with a president, chosen by the federal parliament, replacing the governor-general. In part, the vote failed because some republicans insisted on directly electing a president, on the

Irish model. Mainstream republicans such as Keating and future prime minister Malcolm Turnbull saw a popularly elected president as threatening the basis of parliamentary supremacy.

More likely, the referendum failed because most voters could see no particular flaws in the existing system. As Mark McKenna has pointed out, the monarchist case was essentially negative, with the use of slogans such as *Vote No to the Politicians' Republic* and *Don't Know? — Vote no.* This, as Paul Keating observed, was 'the love that dare not speak its name'.[4] When Tony Abbott, who had led the 'No' campaign, became prime minister in 2013, his restoration of knighthoods, which had been abolished with the establishment of an Australian honours system in 1975, was met with derision, and contributed to his downfall. The confusion among Australian conservatives was symbolised by his replacement by the republican Malcolm Turnbull, who in turn was deposed by his own party within three years.

Republicans complain that the retention of the monarchy means no Australian can become head of state. They point to the absurdity of retaining as sovereign someone on the other side of the world, and the impact that this has on Australia's image, especially in Asia. There are few active republicans in the current Liberal/National government, while the opposition Labor Party remains committed to it in principle. The Australian Republican Movement has avoided committing to any particular process for choosing a president; I would favour a vote of all federal and state

MPs, which would mean a candidate would need to be broadly acceptable across party lines, while retaining the primacy of parliamentary government. The Canadian republican movement is also unclear about how they would choose a head of state, although the website of Citizens for a Canadian Republic suggests that 'this position need not be political or popularly elected'.[5]

The constant media frenzy around the younger generation of the royals has made republicanism a less popular movement in Australia than it was two decades ago. Most of us accept the logic of the argument, without much interest in pursuing it, perhaps because the republican movement doesn't suggest any urgency. In a recent polemic, the historian Benjamin Jones claims that 'Australia is one of the only nations in the world with a constitution that actively discriminates against its own citizens'. (He thus ignores the other dominions and the United States, which requires a president to be 'natural born' and at least thirty-five years old.) But a page later he writes, 'Australia has become republic like without having a republican movement.'[6] In fact, the governor-general, who since 1965 has always been an Australian, performs all the roles of a constitutional head of state. Nonetheless the Queen's image remains on our coins and banknotes; her birthday provides the occasion for a public holiday and a special stamp issue from Australia Post.

The dismissal underlined the ambiguity in the Australian constitution that seemed to give the governor-general greater power than the Queen has in Britain, just as Canadian lieutenant-governors have been more willing to exercise their power in decisions to prorogue parliament than has Queen Elizabeth. There is a tantalising sentence in Malcolm Turnbull's memoirs where he suggests that then governor-general Sir Peter Cosgrove would have refused to prorogue parliament should Turnbull have requested it.[7] During the extensive lockdowns in the state of Victoria because of COVID-19, a former state attorney-general suggested there was a role for the state governor in whether to approve restrictions on freedom of movement.[8]

There are very similar arguments about republicanism in New Zealand, where again popular sentiment and logic tend to conflict, although constitutional change is far easier to achieve there than in the federal systems of Australia and Canada. Nationalist (that is, conservative) prime minister Jim Bolger (1990–97) favoured a republic, and is quoted as saying, 'I have more than once spoken with Her Majesty about my view that New Zealand would at some point elect its own Head of State, we discussed the matter in a most sensible way and she was in no way surprised or alarmed and neither did she cut my head off.'[9] Because of the signing of the Treaty of Waitangi in 1840 between the Crown and the Māori, it is sometimes claimed that many Māori have long-held reservations regarding any move to a republic.

Common sense would suggest that the remaining Commonwealth countries whose head of state is the British sovereign should discard the pretence of monarchy, but the uncertainty of global political change has reduced the likelihood of a change to the system in at least the older dominions. Maybe the strange rituals of a British monarchy have helped some adapt to the rapid demographic changes that have made these countries less and less the imagined outposts of what used to be called 'the home country'. Whatever the reasons, the appetite for abandoning the monarchy seems slight. As the Australian Don Watson, once a strong republican, wrote, 'In a world filling with tyrants, Queen Elizabeth and her descendants represent a sort of anti-tyranny.'[10] His views are supported by Justice Michael Kirby, who wrote:

> The constitutional monarchy remains today as it was in 1949, in Ben Chifley's words, 'a handy constitutional fiction'. The Crown in Australia has lasted from Captain Cook to the so-called Palace Papers. It has saved us from some horrible alternatives. Changing it is not a priority.[11]

At least in Australia, a meaningful recognition of Indigenous Australians and a bill of rights seem more pressing constitutional matters.

# The Commonwealth

The most significant contribution of the Queen may well be as head of the Commonwealth, a term first employed after World War I to replace what had been called the Empire. The Commonwealth is a loose alliance of fifty-three former British colonies, plus several small African countries that have subsequently joined. The Commonwealth engages in a range of low-key initiatives, but also brings together a unique gathering of heads of government every two years, the largest such gathering outside United Nations meetings.

Ever since her royal tour with her parents to South Africa in 1947, Queen Elizabeth has made the Commonwealth a personal priority, and it is possible it might not have survived without her personal commitment. She has been an assiduous champion of Commonwealth links, visiting almost every member state, in several cases against the wishes of the British government. Most controversial was her visit to Ghana in 1961 after Kwame Nkrumah declared the country a republic. The left was shocked by his crack-down on dissent, the right by anti-British sentiments, and there was considerable pressure to cancel the visit. The memoirs of then prime minister Harold Macmillan make it clear that the Queen was determined to go, and that she saw the visit as marking a necessary evolution of the Commonwealth.

As Pimlott demonstrates, the Queen has played a key role in developing the Commonwealth, often having access to political leaders independent of advice from the British government. There was veiled disagreement with Margaret Thatcher over attitudes towards the white government of Southern Rhodesia, and to sanctions against South Africa — the Queen being more sympathetic to African nationalism.[1] In the case of Rhodesia, the position of the Queen had been critical, as the white-settler government pledged their allegiance to her even as they declared unilateral independence, which Britain — and the Queen — did not recognise. The renamed Zimbabwe finally became independent under majority rule in 1980, after a long and bitter struggle, and two decades later withdrew from the Commonwealth after its membership was suspended in 2002 for its failure to ensure basic democratic rights.

Precisely because she was not seen as the effective ruler of Great Britain, former colonies could accept the Queen as the symbol of the Commonwealth. And her support for certain Commonwealth initiatives has at times caused friction with her British government, as in remarks in 1983 that the greatest problem facing the world was 'the gap between rich and poor countries' — not the primary concern of the Thatcher government. At a heads-of-government meeting in 2018, the Queen ensured that, on his accession, Prince Charles would also become head of the Commonwealth, and the royal family still invest considerable effort in building ties across the Commonwealth. Whether the institution would survive a collapse of the British monarchy is hard to estimate; for the small island states of the Caribbean and the Pacific, the Commonwealth is a useful forum a and source of technical assistance.

Few international institutions are as badly understood as the Commonwealth. The Commonwealth manages a number of programs through a London secretariat, but is best known for the Commonwealth Games and the biennial heads-of-government meetings (CHOGM), which have traditionally been chaired by the Queen as head of the Commonwealth. This provides an opportunity for the rulers of small states to meet face to face with heads of government from five of the G20 nations, but it is generally regarded as less significant than regional groupings such as the African Union.

The Commonwealth Charter proclaims that it is committed to 'the development of free and democratic societies and the promotion of peace and prosperity to improve the lives of all the people of the Commonwealth'. Most Commonwealth countries are republics, although some have their own monarchical systems, as in Malaysia,

Tonga, and Lesotho, while the monarchs of Brunei and Eswatini (formerly Swaziland) have retained absolute power. So much for protestations of shared democratic values, although several countries have been suspended for gross violations of democratic principles — twice, in the case of Fiji. In the words of Michael Wesley, 'Today the Commonwealth exists as an organisation in search of a rationale ... Its bonds are not hard objectives of modern statecraft but a subterranean sentimentality of connectedness; it endures in its benignity because no one has the heart to kill it off.'[2]

For many Commonwealth countries, the most obvious connection is through cricket — although, most notably, that excludes Canada. What still connects a number of Commonwealth countries is what they share with the United States, namely the use of English; France has tried to replicate the Commonwealth through the Francophonie, an even less meaningful international organisation. And these ties are not inconsequential; even today, one finds many Asian and African citizens of Commonwealth countries who have grown up reading the books of British childhood, even if it is unlikely that a young Ghanaian, for example, will read the novels of a young Pakistani unless the books have first travelled through London.

There is little evidence that key member states such as India or South Africa have much interest in a stronger institution. But while the ties are fragile, they do allow for connections to be established between countries in very different parts of the world, even if the ambitions of the Commonwealth remain aspirational rather than actual. In the aftermath of Brexit there was some British interest in reviving the Commonwealth, but that discussion was sadly commandeered by people interested in restoring a mythical Anglosphere anchored by the 'old Dominions' — people one commentator described as 'a grim collection of charlatans, chancers and outright villains'.[3] Some of the enthusiasts for Brexit are also arch-monarchists, such as the dandy cabinet minister Jacob Rees-Mogg, who has called for a glamorous monarchy, deserving of yet further support from the public purse.[4] This might seem a perfect example of monarchy as harmless nostalgia, but the high Tory view of monarchy stems from a sense of entitlement that is deeply undemocratic.

# The Europeans

Traditionally, European royal families are interlocked through marriage; the current British, Danish, Greek, Spanish, and Yugoslav (Serbian) families are connected in ways that need a three-dimensional family tree to fully illustrate. Increasingly, though, marrying commoners has become the norm rather than the exception. This is the case for the current kings of Norway, Sweden, and Spain; Mary, the future Queen of Denmark, was an Australian advertising executive; and the wife of the Grand Duke of Luxembourg was a Cuban political-science student. (Even the Japanese emperor is married to a commoner, a former member of the Foreign Office.) Every current European monarch, with the exception of the Ruritanian prince of Liechtenstein, can claim descent from George II of Great Britain, whose descendants also include the deposed royal families of a number of countries, including Greece, Russia, and Romania, and numerous German dukes and princes.

The two great wars of 1914–18 and 1939–45 were major turning points for European monarchies. The Austro-Hungarian, German, and Russian empires collapsed after World War I, the Portuguese monarchy having already been overthrown in the revolution of 1910; following World War II, a plebiscite in Italy saw the end of monarchy; and communist parties replaced monarchies in Bulgaria, Romania, and Yugoslavia. Although Franco had not abolished the monarchy in Spain, he refused to allow the throne to be occupied, and monarchies seemed confined to small countries in the north-west of the continent. Yet in most countries where they remain, there seems little interest in displacing them, and in some cases support for monarchy seems stronger than ever. With the possible exception of Spain, none of the seven republican movements in Western Europe seems capable of building much popular support. Europeans appear to view republicanism as either a harmless foible or a dangerous extremism.

The visibility of George VI and his family as symbols of British resistance during World War II greatly strengthened British support for the monarchy, as did the presence in exile of Queen Wilhelmina of the Netherlands, Grand Duchess Charlotte of Luxembourg, and King Haakon of Norway. As the last generation to remember World War II die, so too does some of the sentimental attachment to the monarchies. The Greek King George II, who had been restored by referendum in 1935, also went into exile, and the monarchy was restored by referendum in 1946 and then abolished by the military coup of 1973; George is reported to have said: 'The most important tool for a King of Greece is a suitcase.' In 1950 Belgium's King Leopold abdicated after a popular vote upheld the monarchy but revealed considerable distrust of Leopold, who was suspected of collaboration with the Germans. (Leopold had remained in Belgium while the then government established itself as a government in exile in London.)

The image of the contemporary monarch, above politics and in close touch with her subjects, is largely based on the seven remaining monarchies of Scandinavia and the Benelux, although Luxembourg is a dukedom rather than a kingdom — and by some estimates the richest ruling family in Europe. Each has its own unique history and political conditions: the Norwegian throne dates back to King Harald in 872, even though the current king is not a direct descendent; the German Leopold I became the first king of the newly independent Belgium in 1831 after turning down the throne of Greece. His family's marriages linked royal houses in Britain, Russia, Portugal, and Bulgaria. It is easier to find information about the monarchies of north-western Europe from the gossip columns than from political-science texts, which suggests they are either totally politically neutered or else their influence is very carefully concealed.

As in Britain, the remaining monarchies have all experienced a steady decline in royal powers since the end of World War II, with occasional exceptions, such as the role played by Juan Carlos of Spain. In his almost forty-year reign, Juan Carlos eased the transition from autocracy to liberal democracy, and went from being a national hero to a disgraced exile.

# Spain and the transition to democracy

During the 1920s Spain fell under the military dictatorship of Primo de Rivera, supported by King Alfonso XIII, who had been monarch since his birth in 1886. Under popular pressure, Rivera resigned in 1930, and the following year Alfonso left Spain, after widespread gains for republican parties in municipal elections, which led to the installation of the Second Spanish Republic. Several years later, the military revolted against the new socialist government, leading to a bitter civil war and the eventual success of General Franco. Under Franco, Spain became a fascist dictatorship, with Franco declaring himself regent while refusing to allow Alfonso or his sons to return to Spain. While Franco was committed to restoring the monarchy, he went to great lengths to exclude the man with the best claim to the throne, Don Juan de Borbon, whom he perceived as far too liberal. Franco even flirted with the possibility of offering the throne to Otto von Habsburg, who had grown up in Spain, but he gradually cultivated Don Juan's elder son, Juan Carlos, who took office two days after Franco's death in 1975. Franco had hoped that Juan Carlos would continue the Falangist policies that had made Spain a fascist dictatorship, but he proved to be more liberal than Franco had foreseen.

In the several years that followed Franco's death, Juan Carlos played a crucial role in the negotiations that led to free elections in 1977 and a new constitution in 1978. Distrusted on the left as a protégé of Franco, and on the right for his commitment to liberal values, the king was the central figure in Spain's transition to liberal democracy. He was assiduous in seeking the support of major Western countries, and his coronation, very soon after Franco's death, was attended by the French and German presidents, US vice-president Rockefeller, and the Duke of Edinburgh. (The Chilean dictator, General Pinochet, in Spain for Franco's funeral, was a conspicuous absence.) In his very admiring biography of Juan Carlos, Paul Preston writes: 'For the next 18 months, Juan Carlos's future would be worked out in a context of drama and conflict on the streets and complex negotiations behind the closed doors of smoke-filled rooms.'[1]

Juan Carlos chose as his transitional prime minister Adolfo Suárez, a former Franco ally who shared the king's vision of liberal democracy. Suárez formed a new Christian Democratic Party that won the 1977 elections, and he remained prime minister for the next four years. As the Cortes were meeting to appoint his successor, members of the Civil Guard entered and proclaimed that they were taking command in the name of the king. The officers held the parliamentarians hostage for eighteen hours, during which time Juan Carlos refused to endorse the coup. In a televised address to the nation, he made clear his commitment to parliamentary government, a speech that the historian Tony Judt suggested showed a courage and determination that surprised most Spaniards.[2] It took some years before the threat of attempted coups by right-wing military officers, including possible assassination attempts against the king, disappeared; and in the first decade after Franco, Spain experienced threats to the new liberal order from sections of the military and the Basque terrorist group ETA.

Juan Carlos's reign ended unhappily with a series of scandals sparked by reports in 2012 of a $46,000 hunting trip — accompanied by a much younger lover, and paid for by a Saudi royal adviser — from which he was flown back to Spain, on a private jet, for emergency surgery. Already it was widely known that he was receiving large sums from Arab autocrats in return for political favours,[3] and in 2014 he abdicated in favour of his son, King Felipe, followed by his eventual departure in 2020 for the United Arab Emirates. His daughter, Princess Cristina, had previously been tried for corruption and found innocent, but her husband was imprisoned; Juan Carlos has now followed Cristina into exile. The antics of Juan Carlos and his daughter have eroded much of the support for the monarchy that was built up during the immediate post-Franco years.

While Spain is a constitutional monarchy, Filipe has been involved more directly in politics than other contemporary European rulers, except those in the tiny principalities of Liechtenstein and Monaco. Political instability after the 2015 elections led to elections the following year, since when Spain has been governed by uneasy coalitions of political parties, first of the right and currently of the left. As in Belgium, the monarch becomes a reluctant referee when the electoral process fails to produce clear results, although it appears that Felipe has acted within the restraints of a constitutional monarch.

Faced with the separatist movement in Catalonia, King Felipe has spoken very strongly against separatism — unlike Queen Elizabeth, who expressed no views in public about either Scottish independence or Brexit. (The closest the Queen came during the 2014 referendum concerning Scottish independence was to say that she hoped the people of Scotland would 'think very carefully about the future'.)[4] While most Scottish Nationalists speak of retaining the Queen as head of state, independence for Catalonia would break with the Spanish crown. A group of parliamentarians from Catalonia, Galicia, and the Basque Country boycotted the opening of the Spanish parliament in 2020 to protest against the king, who has been booed on visits to Barcelona. Similar protests had met Juan Carlos on visits to the Basque Country in the 1980s.

Spain has a strong republican tradition, and public opinion polls reveal considerable, if fluctuating, support for abolishing the monarchy. The ruling Socialist Party is formally committed to a republic, and Podemos, its smaller coalition partner, is strongly republican, but their lack of a clear parliamentary majority makes abolition of the monarchy unlikely in the foreseeable future. In 2020 Felipe renounced any inheritance from the estate of his father, as concerns about financial impropriety still surrounded the Spanish royal family, and observers noted a rise in republican sentiment in Spain.[5]

# The Scandinavians and
## *The King's Choice*

Despite enduring continually changing borders, the three Scandinavian countries all have long traditions of monarchical rule; in the Middle Ages there was a single ruler of the Kalmar Union. After its collapse, Norway came under Danish rule, and then passed to Swedish control in 1814. In both Denmark and Sweden, the spectre of revolution in Russia and the collapse of the German and Austrian empires after World War I saw monarchs accept the primacy of parliamentary government.

After Norway became independent from Sweden in 1905, a referendum adopted a constitutional monarchy, and the Danish prince Haakon was chosen, in part because of his close ties to Danish, Swedish, and British royalty. The three Scandinavian monarchies were tested during World War II; although they made different choices, the brother kings of Denmark and Norway were seen as symbols of resistance to Germany, while Sweden's King Gustav V was suspected of pro-German sympathies, and Sweden remained neutral throughout.

There's a television series called *Occupied* that posits the dilemmas for Norway in a scenario where Russia seeks to take over effective control of the country with the tacit acceptance of the United States and the European Union. The series revolves around the moral dilemmas of collusion, a very real issue in Norway, where a puppet government led by Quisling took power after the German invasion in 1940. Haakon and his family spent the remainder of the war in Britain. The themes of *Occupied* echo the film *The King's Choice*, which counterposes the refusal of King Haakon to surrender with that of his brother, then king of Denmark, Christian X, who remained in Copenhagen throughout the war, but signalled his independence of the occupying German forces by taking daily horse rides through Copenhagen unaccompanied by any guard.

In all three cases the behaviour of the king was crucial, even though each governed a constitutional monarchy. In times of crisis, even a constitutionally restrained head of state needs to act, because not to act will have repercussions. Sweden's King Gustav is alleged to have intervened to allow the Germans to transfer a fighting infantry division through Swedish territory from southern Norway to northern Finland in June 1941, but he also supported providing refuge to Jews from other Scandinavian countries. Like his government, he manoeuvred to preserve Swedish neutrality and to quietly assist the Allies once Hitler's defeat was imminent.

All three monarchs retained their thrones after the war — unlike the situation in the Balkan states, where new communist governments replaced monarchies, giving rise to a whole category of royal pretenders. In Sweden there was considerable debate about the role of the monarchy; it was resolved in 1971 in the Torekov compromise, in which representatives of all political parties except the communists agreed that the monarchy would become entirely ceremonial, without even the residual political powers of other Scandinavian monarchs. The king retains the right to be kept informed of government matters by the prime minister, but has no power over legislation or the choice of ministers. Royal palaces are the property of the state, although the royal family hold several private residences. Since he succeeded in 1974, King Carl seems to have been preoccupied with cars, scouting, and the creation of royal titles for his descendants.

There are republican movements in the three Scandinavian countries, but there seems to be widespread acceptance of the monarchy. In 2019 a bill to abolish the monarchy was heavily defeated in the Norwegian parliament. While without any formal political power, the king meets with the Council of State every Friday, and holds weekly meetings with the prime minister and the foreign minister. Unlike the British, the official royal family is small; even the king's eldest daughter has relinquished her title of 'Royal Highness'.

Denmark today is a small, rich nation with a smaller population than half a dozen European metropolitan areas, but its royal family claim a thousand-year history — a reminder that at one point Denmark dominated the Baltic and had possessions in Africa, India, and the West Indies. Iceland was an independent country from 1918 under the Danish throne, but voted to become a republic in 1944, while Greenland and the Faroe Islands are self-governing within the Kingdom of Denmark.

However accessible the Danish sovereign may be, she is also a symbol of national pride. Queen Margrethe of Denmark has been on the throne for forty years, and she holds orders from thirty countries; she is a Grand Cordon of Abu Dhabi's Order of Al Nahayyan, and a knight of Thailand's Most Auspicious Order of the Rajamitrabhorn.

# The Benelux countries

The three Benelux countries — Belgium, the Netherlands, and Luxembourg — are constitutional monarchies that took their current shape as the result of Great Power negotiations during the early nineteenth century. The Netherlands had been a republic for several hundred years until 1798, although the house of Orange-Nassau, from which the current sovereign is descended, had been a dominant power in the republic. Belgium became a separate state in 1830 after a revolution against the rule of the Dutch King William, and Luxembourg became an independent duchy in 1839, although recognising the sovereignty of the Dutch monarch until 1890. By the early twentieth century all three countries had become constitutional monarchies similar to that of Great Britain, although Queen Wilhelmina of the Netherlands exerted considerable political influence until her abdication in 1948.

Unlike Britain, the Benelux monarchs are limited by

written constitutions: one-third of the Dutch constitution describes the succession, mechanisms of accession to and abdication from the throne; the roles and responsibilities of the monarch; and formal communications between the States General (the Dutch Parliament) and the monarch. Officially, the role of the monarch is to act as a symbol of the nation and as a focal point for social cohesion; as elsewhere, royal families switch effortlessly between charitable works and celebrity scandals.

It is sometimes claimed that the monarchy is the only institution that unites the Flemish and French speakers of Belgium, although the Flemish Nationalist Party, the right-wing Vlaams Belang, advocates a Flemish republic. The royal family are bilingual, but are perceived as French in orientation, even though they have retained the Saxe-Coburg family name, a reminder of their German origins. Claims that the monarch promotes national unity are frequent, but little supported by evidence. As one Belgian political scientist told me:

> What maintains Belgium is public debt, Europe, and, above all, Brussels. Brussels is our richness, our window on the outside world, encircled by Flanders while inhabited by a majority of French speakers. A Flanders that declared independence would lose Brussels.

But the continuity and deference that the monarchy embodies allows for influence even when it is proscribed. As the official government website suggests, echoing Bagehot, the Belgian king exercises his role 'by suggesting, advising, warning and encouraging'. In fact, the Belgian king plays a significant role in forming governments when there is no clear parliamentary majority, and retains the power to veto legislation, although it is very unlikely this power would be used. In 1990 King Baudouin told the prime minister he could not sign a law permitting abortion, albeit with a number of conditions, without violating his conscience as a Catholic, and abdicated for a twenty-four-hour period to allow the bill to pass. A refusal by the Grand Duke of Luxembourg to sign a law mandating euthanasia in 2008 led to a constitutional amendment taking away the need for royal assent.[1]

The very complex politics of Belgium, which are divided along both linguistic and ideological lines, has given King Philippe greater scope to intervene than is usual. Elections for both the federal and regional legislatures were held in May 2019; ten months later, no successful government had been formed, and the outgoing caretaker government had its mandate extended to cope with the outbreak of COVID-19, which hit Belgium particularly hard. In the intervening period, the king became increasingly involved in complex negotiations between the large number of political parties, which were finally resolved in September 2020 with a coalition of centrist and leftist parties. It is unlikely that this will end the Palace's involvement in political deadlocks.

In the Netherlands the powers of the monarch have been gradually whittled down, and since changes in 2012 the king no longer has a significant role in choosing a government following a general election. There are several republican movements, and the Dutch Labour Party (the PvdA), rather like its Swedish counterpart, is largely in favour of abolishing the monarchy, but shows no desire to do so in the immediate future. There have been moments of republican sentiment, most notably in the so-called Coronation Riots of 1980, which coincided with Beatrix's accession to the throne, and again in 2001 when Crown Prince Willem-Alexander announced his engagement to the daughter of a member of the Argentinian military government of the 1970s. On Willem's accession to the throne, Maxima Zorrequieta became the first overseas-born queen of the country. Willem had piloted commercial KLM flights, continuing this on occasion as king.

Even the most scrupulous monarch will be perceived as expressing personal views, however anodyne their comments. In her 2007 Christmas Speech, Queen Beatrix of the Netherlands made comments that were seen by the media as critical of the anti-immigrant policies of Gert Wilders' Freedom Party, who subsequently called for further restrictions on the powers of the monarchy. Similarly, remarks by Queen Margrethe that Danes may have underestimated the difficulties involved in the successful integration of immigrants addressed unease about growing numbers of immigrants, specifically from Muslim countries. And there was considerable attention paid to comments by the King of Sweden in December 2020, when he criticised the government's response to COVID-19, which involved far fewer restrictions — and brought many more deaths — than in neighbouring countries.

How far monarchs actually influence political decisions in the constitutional monarchies of Western Europe is difficult to know. In all cases, the monarch still meets regularly with the prime minister, and in the Netherlands King Willem is part of the Council of State, which must be consulted by the cabinet on proposed legislation before a law is submitted to parliament. His mother, Queen Beatrix, was said to have expressed her views on political developments in meetings with ministers and parliamentarians. Her husband, Prince Claus, held a number of senior semi-government positions that gave him extraordinary access to the workings of government.

# Asian monarchies

While the extant Asian monarchies have all been influenced by European ideas of constitutionalism, there is considerable variety between them, and less commonality than is true of the Europeans. There is far less intermarriage among Asian royalty, but they benefit from the solidarity that exists among all royal families. When the Malaysian king dismissed Mahathir Mohamed in February 2020, Prince Michael of Liechtenstein wrote a defence of the monarch's role on the website of the 'Geopolitical Intelligence Services' — a project of the prince's.[1]

All the Asian monarchies have been shaped to some extent by Western colonialism; only Thailand has resisted both colonialism and defeat in war. The division of the Malay archipelago between the British and Dutch during the nineteenth century produced what we now know as the states of Malaysia and Indonesia; whereas Indonesia adopted a republican form of government after gaining independence in 1949, the Malay sultans, who had survived as rulers of much of the country during British control, have been able to retain their position in a postcolonial Malaysia. Of the former monarchies of French Indochina, only that of Cambodia's survives.

## JAPAN

Japan is the rare example of a defeated country retaining its monarch, even though Emperor Hirohito had been assailed throughout World War II as the principal enemy of the Allies in the Pacific War. It is ironic that it was a decision by the republican United States that maintained what may be the longest-lasting of all royal dynasties — and the only remaining one with the title of emperor.

The Japanese imperial family claim to trace their origins back to Emperor Jimmu, whose accession in 660 BC is seen as the origin of the Japanese Empire. As Jimmu was believed to have been a descendent of the sun goddess Amaterasu, daughter of the gods who created the islands of Japan, the connection is mythological rather than actual, but the importance of the emperor to Japanese national identity is crucial. Ben Anderson noted that 'Japan is the only country whose monarchy has been monopolized by a single dynasty throughout recorded history', but also suggests its origins may have been Korean.[2] The Japanese novelist Mishima, who committed suicide in 1970, did so in honour of the emperor. As recently as 2000, Japanese prime minister Mori referred to Japan 'as a divine country centred on the emperor'.

The American victors in 1945 recognised the importance of the emperor, making the decision to remove his political powers while maintaining him as the symbolic head of state in occupied Japan. The Japanese had done something similar after their annexation of Korea when the Korean imperial House of Yi became members of the Japanese imperial house, and the deposed Korean emperor was given the status of an imperial prince. After World War II, most Japanese imperials lost their status — as did the Korean imperial family.

There is controversy about the role Emperor Hirohito played in Japanese aggression in the 1930s and World War II, but he actively supported many of the decisions taken by his government.[3] After the war, he proved adept in adapting to the new ceremonial role imposed on him by General MacArthur, and was a strong supporter of the United States in the emerging Cold War. Under MacArthur, the Americans not only accepted the continuation of the emperor's position, but went to some lengths to protect other members of his family from prosecution for war crimes. They viewed maintaining the mythology of the imperial family as contributing to the stability of a post-war liberal democracy. The post-war settlement did, however, involve shrinking the size of the imperial family: fifty-one members were formally removed from the imperial household register and became ordinary citizens.

A small group known as Hantenren (Anti Emperor Activities Network) protested for many years against Hirohito, calling for him to be held accountable for war crimes, but there was widespread acceptance of the monarchy, especially after his eldest son, Akihito, succeeded to the throne in 1989. As crown prince, he had already reached out to countries occupied by Japan in World War II, visiting thirty countries and later another twenty-eight, including China, as emperor. His attempts to find meaning in a symbolic role suggested a model for other constitutional monarchs, as John Breen wrote in discussing the emperor's decision to abdicate in 2017 against the wishes of prime minister Shinzo Abe:

> [His] first and foremost duty [was] to pray for [the] peace and happiness of all the people. He insisted, with still greater conviction, on his need to 'stand by the people, listen to their voices, and be close to them in their thoughts'. It was his role to nurture 'deep understanding of the people,' and 'an awareness of being with the people'.[4]

In 2019 Hirohito's grandson, Naruhito, was crowned emperor, and has expressed great remorse for the Pacific War, which Abe never did in his eight years as prime minister. Rather like his British counterparts, Naruhito has complained of media harassment of his wife, Masako Owada.

Not surprisingly, some Japanese see the emperor as an anodyne figure, uneasily suspended between living an essentially bourgeois family life and paying occasional homage to Japan's imperial past. Shortly after he came to the throne, Naruhito performed the secret ritual Daijosai, when the emperor enters a purpose-built shrine to extend gratitude to the gods for good harvest, for the peace and safety of the nation, and also to pay homage to the ancestral gods of the emperor's family. There have been legal challenges to the use of government funds to pay for an expensive religious ceremony — the shrine complex is dismantled after the ritual — in a country that is constitutionally secular. The Japanese ceremony is based on Shinto beliefs, but it has its counterpart in the British coronation ceremony, where the sovereign disappears from public view to be privately anointed.

## MASTER OR CYPHER? THE MONARCHIES OF SOUTH-EAST ASIA

There are four monarchies in south-east Asia, ranging from the despotic in Brunei to the apparently powerless in Cambodia.

### *Malaysia*

The Malaysian king, the Yang di-Pertuan Agong, is chosen by a council comprising the rulers of the nine Malay states that have hereditary rulers, and holds office for five years.

(The states are Johor, Kedah, Kelantan, Pahang, Negeri Sembilan, Perlis, Perak, Selangor, and Terengganu, and exclude parts of Malaysia with large non-Malay majorities.)

The monarchy is part of the complex set of arrangements that maintain Malay — and Islamic — dominance in a country in which they make up just over 50 per cent of the population. Unlike most monarchies, that of Malaysia deliberately symbolises the dominance of one section of the population. Within each state the hereditary sultans still exercise considerable control, often intervening to resolve political tensions or to override elected governments. In some cases, they have chosen chief ministers over the wishes of the majority party and interfered with ministerial appointments.[5] The Sultan of Johor ordered the state assembly to ban e-cigarettes in 2015, and unilaterally banned vaping in 2016. It is also believed that the sultans make skilful use of their position financially, and several sultans have been linked to dubious land deals.

Federally, the Agong's powers are essentially limited to those associated with constitutional monarchs in Europe. Following clashes between the sultans and Dr Mahathir shortly after Mahathir first became prime minister in 1981, the constitution was amended to remove the need for royal assent to legislation, a move opposed by the royal families but eventually adopted and further strengthened by further amendment in 1994. Mahathir, who was prime minister from 1981 to 2003, and again from 2018 to 2020, clashed several times with the hereditary rulers, who had been closer to the disgraced government of Najib Raszak. After Mahathir was re-elected in 2018, the then Agong, Sultan Muhamed of Kelantan, was forced to reverse his initial refusal to accept Mahathir's choice for attorney-general.

But a new king, the Abdullah of Pahang, was installed the following year, and exercised his discretionary powers to replace Mahathir after a week of confusion in early 2020, during which it became unclear whether Mahathir still had majority support in parliament. In an odd power play, Mahathir resigned and then asked to be recommissioned; the king refused, and, after meeting with all members of Malaysia's lower house, appointed his deputy, Muhyiddin Yassin, in what *The Guardian* termed 'a royal coup'. Muhyiddin Yassin is a Malay nationalist with ties to the disgraced former prime minister Najib Razak, and might have appealed more to the Agong than the more multi-racial government of Mahathir. Later that year, Mahathir's former deputy Anwar Ibrahim sought to persuade the Agong that he had the numbers to form a government, but his attempt to produce a majority fizzled out. At the time of writing, Malaysian politics were best characterised as fluid; given shifting alliances amongst parliamentarians, the Agong has considerable discretion in influencing the course of politics.

Malaysians are reticent to discuss the role of the sultans, very conscious of the possible repercussions if one is too outspoken. (The *Sedition Act* has been used to muzzle criticism of the sultans.) Most seem to accept the continuance of the monarchy as necessary; and if they have sometimes resisted limits on their powers, the sultans have largely accepted the rules of constitutional democracy, in some cases acting as 'neutral arbiters during political tumult ... an improbable legitimator of changes'.[6] The unique system of a rotating monarchy is so deeply intertwined with the idea of a Malay nation that it would be a very different country were it to be abolished. Looking across south-east Asia, it is arguable that Malaysia has maintained a more democratic political system than have its neighbours.

## Thailand

Until 1939 Thailand was known as Siam, and from the late eighteenth century has been ruled by the Chakri dynasty, whose interest in learning about the West was the basis for the novel and musical *Anna and the King of Siam*. The boundaries of modern Thailand were created by nineteenth-century monarchs who played off rival French and British imperial rivalries, leading to some loss of territory that is still reflected in border disputes with Cambodia. Thailand has defined itself as a constitutional monarchy since the overthrow of the absolute monarchy in 1932, but has since experienced nineteen attempted coups d'état — twelve of which were successful. Although at times employing the language of constitutional monarchy, King Bhumipol (1946–2016) became central to Thai politics, and intervened on several occasions to support military coups. Thai politics have long been a tumultuous roller-coaster between military dictatorships and semi-democratic governments, in which the influence of the king is central.

During Bhumipol's reign a specifically Thai version of constitutional democracy was developed in which the king is regarded as bound not by the constitution (of which Thailand has had many), but by the concept of *dhamma,* meaning an obligation to follow the path of righteousness. A text published on the sixtieth anniversary of his reign in 2006 claimed:

[D]asarajadhamma or the ten principles of a righteous king are Theravada Buddhism based principles ... the King ... has transformed the ten principles of dasarajadhamma from religious and moral principles into constitutional principles and practice, or convention of the Constitution, of a modern-day democracy, compatible with the principle of constitutional monarchy.[7]

In other words, the king retains the right to overrule both elected and military governments, and in so doing acts in the real interests of the Thai people.

During his seventy-year reign, King Bhumipol both rejected and supported military coups. He supported the military in 1976, when a junta seized power after the slaughter of students at Thammasat University protesting the return of former military ruler Thanom Kittikachorn to Thailand. But he refused to endorse several attempted coups during the 1980s, and in 1992, when there was increasing violence following an election, he urged a return to democratic government, and effectively ousted the military prime minister, Suchinda Kraprayoon. The king's support for the military coups against the popularly elected government of Thaksin Shinawatra in 2006, and again against his sister Yingluck in 2014, made clear the limits to constitutional democracy in Thailand: despite his polling 56 per cent of the vote in 2006, Thaksin's deposition was justified because 'placing the king at the centre of politics is placing morality at the centre of politics'.[8]

King Bhumipol succeeded in making the monarchy central to the economic and cultural life of Thailand, appearing to care for all his people while allowing enormous disparities of wealth from which the royal family themselves benefited. As Unchanam Puangchong wrote, 'The Crown had become an invisible currency for political, business and cultural relations in the Thai kingdom. In national politics the monarchy's support and endorsement were political capital.'[9] The king and his consort, Queen Sirikit, were assiduous in touring the country and promoting local development projects, and their images were ubiquitous across Thailand, appearing on billboards and evening television news broadcasts as regularly as those of the ruling family of North Korea. Increasingly, the king was hailed as a man of unlimited goodness and wisdom, leading to an officially sanctioned reverence for the royal family that has few counterparts except in absolute monarchies.

The Palace stood at the apex of an elite group of military and businessmen, which Duncan McCargo termed a 'network monarchy'; writing in 2005, after landslide electoral victories by Thaksin, he anticipated a decline in royal powers, but the opposite has in fact occurred.[10] Thailand today is a quasi-military dictatorship in which the monarchy is symbolically important, and which benefits from its links to the ruling junta. More than anywhere else Thailand exhibits a combination of royal power and democratic pretensions.

The junta that took power in 2014 has been aggressive in jailing critics of the monarchy, spending hundreds of millions of dollars on a promotional campaign called 'Worship, protect and uphold the monarchy'. The campaign included television commercials, seminars in schools and prisons, singing contests, and competitions to write stories and films praising the king. Clearly, the ruling generals see the monarchy as an essential tool in justifying their continuing hold on power. But the close relationship between the king and the military junta has led to a renewed questioning of the powers of the monarchy, despite Thailand's very strict lèse-majesté laws that can lead to long prison sentences.

Even while supporting the overthrow of elected governments, Thai kings have been celebrated as champions of democracy. The area of Bangkok that surrounds the Democracy Monument, built to commemorate the coup that ended absolute monarchy, has become a centre that depicts successive monarchs as bringers and defenders of Thai democracy.[11] Ignoring the results of a popular election can be justified in the name of 'Thai-style democracy'.

The accession of Bhumipol's son, Vajiralongkong, in 2016 strengthened the autocratic tendencies of the Thai elite, as the king demanded increased powers, and transferred control of a number of royal agencies, including the royal guard, from the state to the monarch. Under these changes, which included substantial holdings in a major industrial conglomerate and Thailand's largest bank, the king became almost certainly the richest reigning monarch, outdoing even the rulers of the United Arab Emirates. His lavish lifestyle, frequent absences from the country, and the elevation of a 'noble consort' — or official concubine — is undermining the reverence that many Thais feel for the monarchy. The German government has expressed concerns at the king exercising control over Thailand while domiciled in Munich.

Continuing pro-democracy rallies in Bangkok that began in August 2020 included calls for limiting the powers of the Palace — demands that spread rapidly through social media. In early 2020 the hashtag #มีกษัตริย์ไว้ทำไม or #WhyDoWeNeedKing was retweeted more than one million times.[12] On 10 August the protesters made ten demands for reforming the monarchy. These included the abolition of the lèse-majesté laws, cuts to the king's budget, a clear delineation between Crown property and the king's personal wealth, and a requirement for the king to be accountable to parliament, as stipulated in the post-revolution constitution of 1932; a plaque, laid symbolically in the

Royal Plaza, read: 'At this place the people have expressed their will: that this country belongs to the people and is not the property of the monarch, as they have deceived us.' Harry Potter costumes evoked the spectre of 'he-who-can-not-be-named' in reference to lèse-majesté laws.

Supporters of the Thai system point to the situation in neighbouring countries — Vietnam, Cambodia, and Myanmar — as evidence that, whatever its defects, their system is superior. How far this view can persist with a far less popular monarch is in doubt. The current Thai king is regarded as a playboy who spends much of his time abroad, but he has exerted considerable influence over the ruling generals, and has expanded royal prerogatives. It is difficult to maintain the argument that Thailand benefits from a system in which the monarchy provides legitimacy to an authoritarian and militarily dominated government, although it is hard to imagine a transition to a more established democratic system without the active support of the king. To date, the Thai parliament, which is essentially controlled by the military, has rejected any moves to curtail the powers of the king, and protestors are being arrested and charged with offences against the monarch. Without a major reversal of position by the King, it is difficult to see a peaceful resolution for Thailand.

## Cambodia

Unlike Thailand, Cambodia was not able to resist European colonisation, and became a French colony in the nineteenth century, retaining the king alongside the emperor of Annam (central Vietnam) and the king of Luang Prabang (later Laos). The French thought that King Norodom Sihanouk would be easily controlled, but after independence in 1953 Sihanouk abdicated in favour of his father to participate in politics, and was elected prime minister. Upon his father's death in 1960, Sihanouk again became head of state, taking the title of prince. Sihanouk allowed the Vietnamese communists to use Cambodia as a sanctuary and a supply route for their armed forces fighting in South Vietnam. In 1970 Sihanouk was ousted by a military coup, and Cambodia fell into civil war, leading to the triumph of the Khmer Rouge in 1975. After their rule ended, Sihanouk was reinstated as king in 1993, but was unable to prevent the increasingly autocratic rule of Hun Sen, and eventually abdicated in 2004. In his final years, Sihanouk spent much of his time in Beijing while issuing statements on Cambodian politics.

While Cambodia has a similar Buddhist tradition to Thailand, its very different history of colonisation, civil war, and brutal governments meant that Sihanouk was unable to establish the monarchy as central to Cambodian politics in the way his near contemporary, Bhumipol, did in Thailand. In Cambodia, the king is elected for life by the Royal Council of the Throne from among the members of the royal families, and in 2004 the throne passed to Sihanouk's eldest son. Norodom Sihamoni, unlike his father, has refrained from exerting political influence, a polite way of noting that he provides legitimacy to an autocratic and repressive government.

Nor is it possible to argue that the pretence of a constitutional monarchy acts as a restraint on the Hun Sen government. The king appears to live a lonely life within the ornate palace grounds of Phnom Penh, and is closely guarded and kept away from media. Opposition politicians in Cambodia have termed Sihamoni a 'puppet king', and have criticised his unwillingness to safeguard democracy. Ironically, the government uses the offence of 'insulting the King' to imprison political opponents, claiming the country is guided by the principles of 'Nation, Religion, King'. Whether future pressures to democratise Cambodia will envision a role for the monarch is an open question.

# Transitional monarchies

In the aftermath of the Arab Spring, James Traub could have been echoing Huntington's 'king's dilemma' when he wrote about Morocco: 'You can have a country governed by deference and awe, or a country governed by equal citizens. There is no third way.'[1] This ignores the possibility that a monarch might voluntarily give up power, so that, as Roger Kershaw suggested in relation to south-east Asia, 'monarchy may offer special assets to a polity in transition towards democracy'.[2] Kershaw saw this as most likely to occur in Thailand, but recent history suggests he may have been overly optimistic. It is unusual for monarchies to cede power without considerable pressure, as the slow battle for parliamentary supremacy in Britain and northern Europe illustrates. His words seem more appropriate in post-Franco Spain, while Japan's adoption of a liberal democracy after World War II was probably facilitated by the decision — made by occupying forces — to retain the emperor, shorn of any political power.

The small Himalayan state of Bhutan is sometimes held up as an example of a monarch voluntarily ceding power without popular pressure. The Wangchuck dynasty, which came to power in the late nineteenth century, has presided over an apparent transition to parliamentary democracy through the constitution of 2008. Despite claims by the Wangchuck dynasty that democratic transition is their gift to the people, some commentators regard it as a semi-authoritarian regime in which democratic rhetoric disguises the family's continuing hold on power.[3] Similarly, the King of Tonga yielded some powers to a partly elected legislature in 2010, which includes some members of the traditional nobility. In the small southern African kingdom of Lesotho, formerly Basutoland, the ruling family ceded political power after a turbulent period following independence from Britain in 1966, which involved several military coups.

These examples are important, because they warn against adopting a triumphalist narrative that assumes the model of constitutional monarchy embedded in northern Europe and Japan is necessarily appropriate elsewhere. Nonetheless, there are several significant countries that could be classified as undergoing a gradual transition from absolute to constitutional monarchies. Across North Africa and the Middle East, the kingdoms of Jordan and Morocco appear less repressive than most of the other countries of the region, although in both cases the monarch retains considerable control. Both countries claim to be constitutional monarchies, and in both the current king claims to have responded to demands for greater democracy. One obvious difference between them and the more oppressive Gulf regimes is that neither country is kept afloat on massive oil reserves, although both have benefited from financial and military assistance from the United States.

In 2011 King Mohammed VI of Morocco won a landslide victory in a referendum on a reformed constitution he had proposed to placate protests as part of the Arab Spring. While the constitution proclaims that '*Le Maroc est une monarchie constitutionnelle, démocratique, parlementaire et sociale*' ('Morocco is a constitutional, democratic, parliamentary, and social monarchy'), the king is legitimised through claims of descent from the Prophet Muhammad, and retains considerable power. There are some parallels to the Thai monarchy in his claims to embody religious and national identity, and in his enormous wealth, which have helped maintain his rule.

Morocco has a number of political parties, and a government headed by a prime minister who is answerable to the parliament. The king, however, retains control of appointments to the Supreme Court. King Mohammed has been very clever in promoting an image of himself as an enlightened ruler while retaining ultimate control of the country; as one commentator put it, 'The king is good while the politicians are bad.' He has close ties to the Spanish royal family, referring to King Juan Carlos as Uncle Juan, but in language that echoes the defenders of the Thai monarchy, he has said that 'Morocco has a lot to do in terms of democracy. The daily practice of democracy evolves in time. Trying to apply a Western democratic system to a country of the Maghreb, the Middle East, or the Gulf would be a mistake. We are not Germany, Sweden, or Spain.'

Sadly, Morocco appears to be moving towards greater repression, with his critics accusing the king of behaving like an absolute monarch.

Jordan's monarch also claims descent from the prophet Muhammad, his family having been central to the creation of both Jordan and Iraq after the collapse of the Ottoman Empire. In 2012, in response to protests during the Arab Spring, King Abdullah replaced his prime minister and introduced a number of reforms, including laws governing public freedoms and elections. Proportional representation was reintroduced to the Jordanian parliament, a move that he said would eventually lead to parliamentary government. The king still controls the executive, and appoints members of the upper house; as one observer wrote, his response to growing tensions is 'to temporize, introduce cosmetic reforms, and dismiss the government'.[4] The fragility of Jordan, which has more refugees per capita than any other country in the world, and is wedged within the most volatile part of the Middle East, means it is unlikely the king will abandon control.

The *Economist*'s Democracy Index regards Morocco as a hybrid democracy, and Jordan as authoritarian. The World

Press Freedom Index, a project of Reporters Without Borders, rates both Jordan and Morocco ahead of India and Mexico, which are formally full democracies.

Among the emirates of the Persian Gulf, the most likely to move towards some form of constitutional monarchy is Kuwait, whose ruling emir does not have absolute powers; in fact, the elected National Assembly has the authority to remove an emir from his post. Kuwait is the only Gulf State that Freedom House ranks as 'partly free', but at the time of writing a new emir had succeeded — at the age of eighty-three — so it is difficult to predict what might develop. There are no signs of significant reform in either the United Arab Emirates or Saudi Arabia; in the latter, the king has absolute power, limited by constant tensions within the very extended royal family and the powers of fundamentalist imams.

# Why do they survive?

This book began as a conversation with the editor Jakob Horstmann, during which we mused on the strange persistence of monarchies in seemingly progressive democratic states. Of the top ten countries listed as most democratic in *The Economist*'s 2020 survey, only two are not constitutional monarchies: Ireland and Iceland, both of which broke away from imperial bonds last century. As a convinced republican, this led me to explore the proposition that perhaps there was an argument for hereditary heads of state. Of course, correlation is not causation, and any generalisations across countries with very different cultural and economic conditions need to be cautious.

A serious discussion of monarchy in the contemporary world is difficult. The left dislike any remnant of inherited authority; the right imbues it with spiritual significance. The extravagance of many royal families, and the media frenzy surrounding royal events, is distasteful, as is the frequency of scandal and corruption. As Thomas Paine wrote: 'to be a king requires only the animal figure of a man — a sort of breathing automaton. This sort of superstition may last a few years more. But it cannot long resist the awakened reason and interest of man.'

Paine wrote this in 1791: over two hundred years later, we are still waiting for 'awakened reason and interest'. Rather like the death of religion, which rationalists confidently predicted over many decades, monarchy has proven far more resilient than its critics expected. Like religion, it appeals to the emotions and is not easily displaced by reason.

The strongest argument for a hereditary head of state is continuity and a faith that growing up within a palace equips future sovereigns in particular ways, despite all the obvious examples where this is clearly not the case. Royalty is assumed to somehow be beyond politics and an embodiment of 'the nation': even the Scandinavian monarchs grow up surrounded by deference, often more so abroad than at home. As Ed West wrote, 'The advantage of monarchy is that, although it's essentially reactionary, in its modern constitutional form it's ersatz reaction ... it takes all those things we miss from the past, the sense of community, certainty and common ritual, but without the actual horror of the past.'[1]

The most important philosophical defence of monarchy came from the German philosopher Hegel, whose writings have continued to influence very different philosophical traditions. While his writings on monarchy are based on his experience of nineteenth-century Europe, and hardly fit contemporary expectations of democracy, they provide a justification that royalists might well ponder. To quote one exegesis of Hegel:

> Hegel argues that the essential function of a modern European monarch is to legitimize each act of state by adding to it the authoritative approval of the sovereign. His qualification for the job is his birth into the ruling family; his right to rule does not rest on any particular abilities. Nor does he depend on the will of any other individual for his position, as governors-general and ceremonial presidents depend on elected party leaders for their power. The acceptance of primogeniture succession completely removes the crowning of a modern monarch from the sphere of human choice. The monarch owes his position only to nature. The monarch's impartiality is a little more difficult to explain. Hegel's king is no absolute monarch ... By depoliticizing (or depersonalizing) the regime at the top, the monarch creates the conditions in which freedom of political association and competition can continue without disturbing the general rational administration of the state.[2]

There is an echo of Hegel's arguments in comments by the British sociologist Chris Rojek that the paradox of democracy is that, while claiming to extend equality and freedom to all, it 'cannot proceed without creating celebrities who stand above the common citizen and achieve veneration and god-like worship'.[3] In an age battered by constant social media, perhaps the real attraction of monarchy is that royalty need not aspire to their position; as Shakespeare's Malvolio said, 'Some are born great, some achieve greatness, and others have greatness thrust upon them.' Being a celebrity is increasingly an asset in winning political office in the modern age — one thinks of Ronald Reagan and Donald Trump in the United States, but also of business magnates such as Silvio Berlusconi, former television stars such as President Zelensky in Ukraine, or former boxer, now senator, Manny Pacquiao in the Philippines. But while celebrities may make good politicians, they rarely are competent executives.

Royalty combines celebrity, wealth, and nostalgia: almost all surviving monarchies are based on memoires of lost grandeur, evident in the elaborate ceremonies that surround the crowning of a new monarch. Where it survives, monarchy helps perpetuate social hierarchies, although no other democracy has as entrenched a feudal remnant as the House of Lords. In countries with elaborate aristocratic ranks — Britain, Thailand, Malaysia — their status is inevitably linked to the continuation of the monarchy. But even in as egalitarian a country as Denmark there is evidence that proximity to the royal court brings social and economic capital.

The belief that the monarchy embodies some mystical

sense of the nation underlies popular support for the extraordinary elaborate British monarchy, as Tom Nairn argued thirty years ago. Nairn ended his book with the hope that Great Britain would break up into smaller republics, thus pointing to the reality that in Britain, Canada, Spain, and Belgium, monarchies represent a national unit that is bitterly contested by separatist movements.

There is a strong element of inventing historical memory in the persistence of monarchy, whether it be through claims of unbroken, even semi-divine, lineage, as in Japan or Morocco, or past glories, when Danish or Khmer kingdoms held far greater sway than they do now. (At one point, Angkor was one of the largest pre-industrial cities in the world.) The Grand Duke of Luxembourg can look back to a family that was one of the most important political forces in the fourteenth century; the appearance of Norway's royal family on the palace balcony on National Day can symbolise the long history of Norwegian nationalism, even if the reign of the current family only dates back to the beginning of last century. The persistence of monarchy is central to the myth of the eternal nation, even if their medieval ancestors had very different concepts of their realms to the present. Even where monarchies have been abolished, governments extol their memory as part of nation-building, as in the memorials to former Burmese kings in the military government's new capital of Nyapidaw, or Vietnam's creation of the old imperial palace of Hue as a tourist attraction.[4]

It has become a truism to note that the royal panoply has helped Britons adjust to the collapse of their imperial grandeur. The British royals sit at the apex of a massive nostalgia industry, reflected in the continuing attraction of costume-drama television and the books of Agatha Christie. Memories of empire are preserved in the range of honours handed out by the Queen — effectively by her prime minister. (An Indian friend of mine was absurdly proud of being awarded an Order of the British Empire.) But this is a comparatively harmless nostalgia, set against the belligerent demands to return to an imagined past that featured in Donald Trump's calls to make America great again. It reaches its most absurd lengths in those countries that retain the Queen as head of state, even while viewing Britain as a foreign country. My passport, for example, is issued by Australia's governor-general in the name of the Queen, but I still need to join the foreigners' queue at Heathrow.

Support for the monarchy touches on emotional attachments to outdated notions of nation and family, but those dynasties that have survived show great flexibility in adjusting to changing mores. A clumsy monarch can jettison the throne; as Simon Jenkins argued:

> We would not invent [the monarchy] if it did not exist, if only because its essence lies in encapsulating a nation's continuity over time, which a family is uniquely positioned to do. I would not try to 'justify' this. But

politics is about more than reason. Where monarchy exists, as in Britain, it carries advantages. Just as a monarch is lucky in inheriting a throne, so a nation is sometimes lucky in inheriting a monarch.[5]

In his study of Queen Elizabeth, Ben Pimlott dismisses most of the arguments in defence of monarchy, but suggests it might yet represent those most overlooked by mainstream politics: 'The institution might build on its historic role as protector of the unrepresented.' This is also the argument advanced by that indefatigable American defender of monarchy, Frank Pochaska, who extols the monarchy's role in promoting philanthropy.[6] There is something odd in suggesting that a highly pampered aristocratic family can champion the poor and the dispossessed, despite royal patronage of multiple good causes, and occasional interventions, such as Charles's Prince's Trust or Diana's campaign against landmines. Yes, royalty serves to give some sense of belonging to people who feel forgotten by the major institutions of the state, but royal charity is usually carefully calculated not to upset the status quo.

A more indirect but intriguing defence of royalty has been advanced by the American political scientist Eileen McDonagh, who suggests that 'monarchical legacies teach people to view the state as responsible for the welfare needs of the disadvantaged', drawing on the historical view of the monarch as the parent of his people.[7] Maybe this is the view of an American looking enviously at the stronger welfare states of northern Europe, but there is some historical basis for her argument. In rich democratic societies, it is possible to see the monarchy as implicitly resisting the harder edges of neoliberal policies, most obviously in some of the remarks of Prince Charles and Queen Margrethe. Elsewhere, monarchs have learnt to show concern while carefully guarding their wealth and privileges. King Bhumipol built popular support by his relentless advocacy for rural development projects, though without risking any redistribution of wealth; a website, tellingly titled 'Bornrich', claims that the king of Morocco 'has earned the title "guardian of the poor" for making the fight against poverty his priority among all other duties'.

The awkward reality, as Tom Nairn wrote thirty years ago, is that constitutional monarchies survive because they are liked: 'People enjoy the monarchical twaddle, and show very little sign of being robotized or "brain-washed". They relish the weird mixture of cheap fun, exalted moments and great spectacles ...'[8] As one left-wing Dutch site lamented, 'There has been a political crisis in the Netherlands for years, as most Dutch people have lost confidence in the main political parties. In the 21st century, more Dutch people trust the monarchy than the main political parties.'[9] Polls across the globe show declining trust in politicians, which makes the republican alternative increasingly less attractive.

The increasingly polarised nature of politics across much of the world makes the popular election of a president who is supposed to stand above politics more problematic: this is the strongest argument that royalists mount against calls for a republic. Echoing Hegel, they claim that a monarch is prepared from birth to stand outside politics. This gives rise to romanticised views, such as that of the Belgian historian Francis Balace, who claimed, 'In the face of politicians who are more and more discredited, the king has the advantage of being the only man who can swear that his own interests coincide with those of the country.'[10]

It might be more accurate to say that the interests of the monarch are to perpetuate the privileges of his family while persuading the people that it is also their family. Contemporary autocrats also promote their families, but their dynasties tend not to extend beyond one generation, whereas royal families draw legitimacy from extended ancestry. For a nation, the royal family stands as a shared link that cuts across political divisions, a continuing family drama in which we can all take part. We can rejoice when they are happy, and take comfort when their failings suggest that they, too, are fallible human beings. In an interview marking forty years on the Danish throne, Queen Margrethe said:

> The most important thing for me and my family is to try to be a unifying factor for our country and our people. To help to determine who we all are. Hopefully something — that although we do not have an active political role — people trust and feel — yes, is inclusive for them to be part of it all. That we belong together.[11]

Talking to people who live in several constitutional monarchies, it becomes clear that many of us are rational republicans but emotionally attached to the institution, in ways that are often embarrassing to acknowledge. Perhaps the strongest defence that can be made is effectively a negative one: the presence of a monarch is a check on the behaviour of politicians. This assumes that the monarch herself respects the limits of her authority and is prepared to abdicate if she falls out of favour, as was the case with Juan Carlos of Spain.

Arguably, it is the inexorable reality of heredity that underlines the continuing grip of monarchy in so many societies. In a perceptive article on the Australian republican debate, Judith Brett wrote, 'Monarchy symbolises the acceptance of the inevitable limits of mortality as much as the contingent limits of society. It is the deep implication of hereditary monarchy with fate that ... grounds our imagined political community in the real.'[12] Although he grew up under the Habsburg monarchy, Freud was remarkably reticent about commenting on monarchy, though there is a passing reference to the 'loyal inhibition' in his discussion of the importance of religion. His disciple Ernest Jones was more forthcoming. Writing of the 'remarkable interest the majority of people take in the minute doings of royalty', he suggested, 'In the august stateliness and ceremonial pomp their secret daydreams are at last gratified, and for a moment they are released from the inevitable sordidness and harassing exigencies of mundane existence.'[13]

Freudian analyses are no longer fashionable, but they offer interesting insights into the attraction of strong leaders and the need for symbolic figures to whom we can attach ourselves. We may not agree with Jones, who argued that '[i]t is impossible to abolish idea of kingship in one form or another from the hearts of men', but psychoanalytic writings, especially Freud's essays such as *Group Psychology and the Analysis of the Ego* and *Civilisation and Its Discontents*, which seek to explain the psychological underpinnings of political authority, have a new salience in the current world. Freud wrote these essays in the aftermath of World War I, in a Europe that was experiencing a rise of xenophobia and charismatic leaders. We do not need to accept Freud's concepts of libido and sexual repression to recognise the importance of deep-seated emotional needs in political movements that cannot simply be explained by self-interest or utilitarian calculation. People may no longer go to war in the name of their king, but monarchies provide emotional connections to the nation that remain deep, even in liberal democracies. It is not accidental that monarchs long presented themselves as the fathers and mothers of their people, even if that language is increasingly archaic in the case of constitutional monarchies.

In an age when liberal democracy appears to be increasingly threatened, is it possible that the anachronism of a hereditary monarchy provides a buffer against the worst excesses of authoritarian populists? Does a head of state not chosen by politicians provide an alternative symbol of legitimacy to the declining moral authority of parliaments and governments? Populist leaders create strong emotional responses among their followers, which might be harder to arouse when a hereditary head of state acts as a balance. Much as we might deplore the undemocratic nature of monarchy, is it less damaging than the illiberal forms of democracy that are now on the rise globally? If we crave 'bread and circuses', the perpetuation of royal sagas may be less harmful than the fantasies of autocratic rulers.

During World War II, George Orwell mused that the existence of the monarchy might ensure 'a Hitler or a Stalin cannot come to power', arguing that the function of the monarch is to act as 'an escape-valve for dangerous emotions'.[14] Orwell's words were echoed by Ernest Bevin, Labour foreign secretary after World War II, who mused in similar fashion that:

> It might have been far better for all of us not to have destroyed the institution of the Kaiser after the last war — we might not have had this one if we hadn't done so. It might have been far better to have guided the Germans to a constitutional monarchy rather than leaving them without a symbol and therefore opening the psychological doors to a man like Hitler.[15]

This seems a plausible argument, but there are few examples of monarchs supporting genuine democratisation in the absence of popular pressure. Orwell and Bevin might have looked at other countries in inter-war Europe where monarchs colluded with attacks on democratic systems. The presence of an Italian king did nothing to stop the rise of Mussolini, even though some of his advisers wanted Victor Emmanuel to declare martial law to stop the rise of fascism. Had Victor Emmanuel been more committed to maintaining constitutional democracy, the history of Italy could have been very different. Equally, King George II of Greece supported the Metaxas dictatorship in the years leading up to World War II, which helps explain later Greek hostility to the monarchy.

In one of the few serious contemporary analyses of constitutional monarchy, the Swedish economist Christian Bjørnskov has suggested that monarchies help favour trust in the political system, an even more important consideration than it was when he wrote his paper in 2006:

> There may be positive effects of having a lasting role model in the monarch and his or her family, and the existence of a monarch could also ... provide a measure of social and political stability that could influence the formation and stability of generalized trust. Conversely, having official recognition of a royal or imperial family in the 21st century might simply be an indication of some deeper cultural factor that affects both the trust level and has allowed for monarchical institutions to survive.[16]

A wise monarch, committed to democratisation, might indeed help foster greater participation and trust in politics. But it is more likely that those countries that have developed genuine constitutional monarchies have for the most part done so because of the deeper underlying cultural and political conditions to which Bjørnskov refers.

There is no guarantee that even existing monarchies will survive. As *The Times* editorialised after the disgrace of Juan Carlos, 'As Britain's Queen has so often demonstrated, that stability stems not just from the constitutional arrangements but the character of the person occupying the throne. That's a lesson that Spain's monarchy forgets at its peril.'[17] Growing discontent with the Thai monarch may well see considerable changes in the coming years, unless the king reverses his grab for yet more power and wealth. The kings of Jordan and Morocco may fail to maintain their dynasties in the face of new demands for greater democratisation, and the absolute rulers of the Persian Gulf may yet be toppled by another Arab Spring.

# Do we need a head of state at all?

We expect two things of a head of state: to represent the nation symbolically, and to act as the final arbiter if the political process fails. All parliamentary systems need to find ways to balance the role of head of state and head of government, and defenders of constitutional monarchy argue that this provides a better balance than a figurehead president who cannot guarantee the continuity implicit in a hereditary head of state.

Continuity is not always a blessing. Musing on the survival of monarchies in the modern world, *The Economist* opined:

> One of democracy's many virtues is that the institution refreshes its personnel constantly, so its survival does not depend on the performance of an individual. A monarchy's does, for the office may be held by the same person for decades. And the selection process often

throws up candidates too stupid, too corrupt or too arrogant to do such a difficult job. The surprising survival of monarchies is in part a tribute to the nous of the old guard, who have understood the need to subsume their interests into those of the institution. If some of the new bloods fail to learn that lesson, the monarchy may resume its decline.[1]

A monarchy looks backwards; an elected president offers renewal. Yet at a time when liberal democracy seems under assault from all sides, maybe we need to reflect on the virtues of constitutional monarchy for the reasons that Bagehot identified 150 years ago — namely, the advantage of separating actual and symbolic power. In times of uncertainty, many feel a powerful need to identify with an idea or a vision that is personified in the figure of a political or religious leader. The crowds who cheer Donald Trump or Jair Bolsonaro are frightening reminders of the strength of the irrational in politics.

The reluctance of so many defenders of liberal democracy to do away with a monarchical head of state rests upon more than a rational assessment of constitutional balances. Even Norman Baker, whose recent book dissects the abuses by royalty of their privileges in the course of 400 pages, ends by advocating exchanging 'our imperial monarchy for a modern bicycling alternative'.[2] Is there an unrecognised fear that to remove the monarchy is to create a void that would be filled by autocratic rulers?

It is tempting to suggest abolishing the idea of a head of state altogether, which is to take seriously the idea that sovereignty rests with the people. The best example of how this might function comes from Switzerland, where the Federal Council, which is elected by the parliament, doubles as a collective head of state and head of government. The president of the confederation has no powers over and above the other six councillors, and continues to head one of the government ministries. Traditionally, the duty rotates among the members in order of seniority. The closest parallel to this exists in San Marino, which rotates two Captains Regent every six months. However, as the population of San Marino is around 34,000, it is hardly a viable model for other states.

It is surprising how little the Swiss model is mentioned in republican arguments, although one critic of the Canadian monarchy did suggest that there was no longer a need for even a ceremonial head of state: 'The position is a muddled anachronism, a colonial holdover from the age in which Canadian self-government could exist only with a governor's permission, now retconned as a font of checks and balances that are never exercised precisely because the position is regarded as silly and illegitimate.'[3]

I am not persuaded that this is a feasible model in larger countries with different political cultures. (Interestingly, Switzerland is the only significant contemporary nation that has no history of monarchy.) Switzerland's self-image as neutral in all conflicts means there is less need for a symbol of the country who can win coverage in the global media. Without a head of state, the temptation for a head of government to claim imperial trappings becomes greater. That a constitutional monarch rarely intervenes in cases of political impasse might suggest the role is unnecessary: there are cases where the monarchy has acted to preserve democracy, as in Spain in 1977; cases where its impact is ambiguous, as in Malaysia in 2020; and cases where it has been generally regarded as unfortunate, as in Australia in 1975. But the paradox is that while we may be reassured by the possibility that a monarch can act, in most cases the monarchy will be weakened if he or she does. In the end, the existence of a constitutional monarch is a silent brake on the tendency of governments to act autocratically.

It is possible to imagine a system similar to the Swiss in the small countries of northern Europe; it is revealing that in the gripping Danish political television series *Borgen*, the prime minister is at one point referred to, inaccurately, as the head of state, and the monarch never appears. In practical terms, an absence already exists in Canada, Australia, and New Zealand, where the governors-general have neither royal celebrity nor political power. It is harder to imagine doing away with a head of state in countries with considerable internal tensions and inequalities, which is why the potential transition to democratic constitutionalism is such a challenge for countries such as Thailand and Jordan, where the monarchs face Huntington's dilemma of how to preserve their dynasty in the face of popular demands to relinquish power, even if the current Thai king seems unaware of the predicament. And to abolish the monarchy in countries such as Britain, Spain, Belgium, and Malaysia would threaten the precarious unity of the nation-state itself.

Autocrats succeed by presenting themselves as embodiments of the nation, often defined by the exclusion of others — Muslims in India, gypsies and refugees in Hungary, presumed drug dealers in the Philippines. If there is a need for individuals to represent national identity, it is preferable that they are without real power, which is the case for constitutional monarchs. Of course, that defence collapses in the overseas dominions; it is hard to see how a family ensconced in Britain can represent Papuan or Jamaican national identity. And if the 'old dominions' need symbols of nationhood, these are better sought in indigenous memories rather than in the history of the British royals.

Monarchy is, in principle, indefensible for anyone who believes in democratic values, and its abolition is part of the platform of most left parties. Yet it remains deeply entrenched and popular in a number of states that rate highly on most measures of democracy. Countries need both national symbols and political umpires, and the hereditary principle seems to satisfy both needs in a range of countries. Whether monarchies contribute to political stability and openness, or rather persist through inertia and a love of celebrity, remains unanswered. I recognise that models which have been appropriate in rich and largely homogenous Western European countries need to be rethought in very different cultural and political contexts. But the persistence of constitutional monarchy suggests it is an institution that reveals more about the possibilities of politics than either dedicated monarchists or republicans acknowledge.

# A final note

My generation of Australians grew up with images of royalty: the Coronation of Elizabeth II (1952), the Royal Visit (1953), and the constant stories in women's magazines, then found in almost every household. The existence of the monarchy became significant several times in my adult life, caught in Whitlam's famous words after his dismissal: 'Well may we say God Save the Queen. Because nothing will save the Governor-General.' (His words are echoed in the title of this book.) The Whitlam government replaced imperial honours with an Australian system of awards, though it was not until 1984 that 'God Save the Queen' ceased to be our national anthem. Like millions of others, I voted for a republic in 1999 and was disappointed when the referendum failed.

But, caught up in gay and leftist politics, I rarely thought of monarchy, and when I did it seemed largely irrelevant. Writing this book has forced me to think through just why monarchies persist, and whether they are more than extravagant nostalgia for an imagined past.

I wish I could end with either a ringing denunciation of hereditary monarchy, or perhaps a strong affirmation of the continuing wisdom of Bagehot's prescriptions for constitutional monarchy. Instead, I end with some unease. It seems counterintuitive to look to a hereditary monarchy to defend egalitarianism, yet there seems to be some evidence to suggest this is the case. I would certainly argue strongly for the advantages of a nonpartisan and largely ceremonial head of state, although this can be achieved without assuming a hereditary succession.

The only good argument I can see for constitutional monarchy is as a rein on the pretensions of autocratic leaders. When I explained my project to sceptical friends, I would summarise it with the question: would a President Boris be worse than a Prime Minister Boris? In a time of populist autocracies, a constitutional monarch is attractive because she may check the pretentions of political leaders.

I am not a monarchist, as that term is usually deployed, and I shrink from people who so identify themselves. But Spain's example suggests that there is still a role for a monarch in countries where there are popular movements demanding greater democracy. The sad history of Juan Carlos also suggests that too many royals behave appallingly. The monarch who helped open his nation to greater democracy is ending his life in disgrace and exile.

As I write these words, repression is increasing in

Thailand, where a woman has been sentenced to forty-three years' imprisonment for insulting the king. It is hard to see the rulers of Thailand recognising the need to democratise and create a genuine constitutional monarchy. But it is likely that any transition to a more genuinely democratic system can only come about with the support of the monarchy. In a private discussion, a very senior former Thai diplomat spoke of the way the relations between sovereign and prime minister are depicted in *The Crown* as an important lesson for Thailand's democracy movement.

Every monarchy is a product of particular historical circumstances, and I am not foolhardy enough to predict the future for royalty across the world. As an Australian, I find the continued sovereignty of the House of Windsor absurd, but Australia's failure to abandon the British monarch — and the low level of support for constitutional change that currently exists — suggests that constitutional monarchies, once established, are difficult to abandon.[1] Unless a move to republicanism also settles the unresolved issue of Indigenous sovereignty, it would be a largely meaningless gesture. But I suspect the combination of distrust in politicians and widespread fondness for pomp and ceremony will assure the continuation of monarchies well into this century.

# Acknowledgements

I owe special thanks to Jakob Horstmann, who was crucial to the birth of this project, to Wendy Mee and Carolyn D'Cruz, who read drafts and pointed out errors and non sequiturs, and to the La Trobe University Library, which provided continuing support throughout the stringent lockdowns of 2020. And thanks to Henry Rosenbloom at Scribe, a fellow republican, who saw the possibilities of this idea, and responded with grace and alacrity too rare in modern publishing.

A number of people gave me wise advice and input along the way, including Robert Aldrich; Niko Besnier; Frank Bongiorno; Dan Bray; Judith Brett; Eric Campbell; Alonso Casanueva Baptista; Laura Clancy; Fernando Martinez Coma; Michael Connors; Alexander Davis; Andrea Goldsmith; Ahmad Fauzi Abdul Hamid; Robert Horvath; Peter Jackson; Robin Jeffrey; Justice Michael Kirby; Andre Krouwel; Paul Lehmann; Rachael Le

Mesurier; Eileen McDonagh; Amrita Malhi; Jes Fabricius Moller; Mark Pendleton; Marian Pitts; Sir Paul Preston; and Caroline Sagesser.

# Notes

## Introduction

1   Quoted by Jeremy Paxman, *On Royalty*, Viking 2006: 7
2   Jeremy D. Mayer & Lee Sigelman, 'Zog for Albania, Edward for Estonia, and monarchs for all the rest?', *PS: Political Science and Politics* 31:4, 1998
3   Craig Brown, *Ma'am Darling*, Fourth Estate 2017: 247
4   Ben Pimlott, 'The Golden Jubilee', *The Independent*, 2 June 2002

## What is a constitutional monarchy?

1   Karl Popper, 'The Open Society and Its Enemies Revisited', *The Economist*, 23 April 1988
2   Adam Gopnik, 'The General Will', *The New Yorker*, 20 August 2018: 68
3   For insights into the decline of absolute monarchy, see J. Geering et al. 'Why Monarchy? The rise and demise of a regime type', *Comparative Political Studies*, July 2020: 1–38
4   Samuel Huntington, *Political Order in Changing Societies*, Yale University Press 1968: 177
5   *Political Order in Changing Societies*, 179

## Monarchy and colonialism

1   J. C. Sharman, *Empires of the Weak*, Princeton University Press 2019: 50

## Reviving the monarchy?

1    David Motadel, 'What Do the Hohenzollerns Deserve?', *New York Review of Books*, 26 March 2020: 27

2    See www.ethiopiancrown.org/negarit.htm

3    'Ethiopians for Constitutional Monarchy: Our Preamble, Our Promise and Our Policies', https://www.facebook.com/ethiopiansforceconstitutionalmonarchy, 5 June 2019

## Royals as celebrities

1    Martyn Rady, *The Habsburgs*, Allen Lane 2020: 277

2    Anne Wolden-Raethinge, *Queen in Denmark*, English translation, Gyldendal 1989

3    Arianne Chernock, 'The Persistence of Monarchy', *Public Books*, 9 May 2012

4    *On Royalty*, 279

5    Roland Barthes, 'The "Blue Blood" Cruise' in *Mythologies* Vintage 2009: 23

6    Joseph Nye, *Soft Power*, Public Affairs 2004: x

7    Joseph Nye, 'The Infant Prince George Is a Source of Real-World Power', *Financial Times*, 4 July 2013

8    Aziz Chahir, 'Morocco's Mohammed VI: Is his son ready for the crown?', *Middle East Eye,* 18 August 2020

9    F. L. Mueller & H. Merkens (eds), *Royal Heirs and the Uses of Soft Power in Nineteenth-Century Europe*, Palgrave 2016

10   Frances Welch, *Imperial Tea Party*, Short Books 2018: 86

11   Takashi Fujitani, 'Electronic Pageantry and Japan's "Symbolic Emperor"', *The Journal of Asian Studies* 51: 4, November 1992

12   Frederic Deborsu, *Question(s) Royale(s)*, Broche 2012

13   For a recent summary, see Lauren Collins, 'Royal Pains', *The New Yorker*, 21 May 2018

## Institutions matter

1    Hannah Arendt, *On Revolution*, Viking 1965: 150

2    Akhilesh Pillalamarri, 'Why Monarchies Are Still Relevant and Useful', *The Diplomat*, 24 June 2014

3    Roger Scruton, 'A Focus of Loyalty Higher Than the State: the monarchy created peace in Central Europe, and its loss precipitated 70 years of conflict', *Los Angeles Times*, 16 June 1991

4    A. Stepan, J. Linz & J. Minoves, 'Democratic Parliamentary Monarchies', *Journal of Democracy* 25: 2, April 2014

5    Ben Pimlott, *The Queen*, Harper Press 2012: 434

6    Anthony Sampson, *Who Runs This Place? The anatomy of Britain in the 21st Century*, John Murray 2004: 87–91

7    Paul Waldman, 'Trump Keeps Claiming He's a King. The Courts Keep Telling Him He's Not', *Washington Post*, 27 November 2019

8    Mahendra Prasad Singh, 'Constitutionalism and State Structure', in H. Roy & M. P. Singh (eds), *Indian Political Thought: themes and thinkers*, Noida: Pearson India Education Services 2019: 354.

9    Eric Hobsbawm, 'What's the Point of the Monarchy?', *Prospect*, 23 March 2011

10   Philip Murphy, *The Empire's New Clothes: the myth of the Commonwealth*, Oxford University Press 2018: 99

11   Norman Baker, *And What Do YOU Do?*, Biteback Publishing 2020: 392

12   George Bernard Shaw, *The Apple Cart*, Penguin Books 1958: 8

# Royal fluffery

1    David Cannadine, 'The British Monarchy' in E. Hobsbawm & T. Ranger, *The Invention of Tradition*, Cambridge 1983: 161

2    Quoted by Julia Baird, *Victoria: The Queen*, Random House 2016: 486

3    *And What do YOU Do?*, 58

4    Andrew Marr, *The Diamond Queen*, Pan Books 2012: 142

5    *The Queen*, 335

6    Laura Clancy, 'The Corporate Power of the British Monarchy', *Sociological Review*, 21 April 2020

7    'Harry, Meghan and Marx', *The Economist*, 16 January 2020

8    'Royals Vetted More Than 1,000 Laws via Queen's Consent', *Guardian*, 9 February 2021

9    Robert Lacey, 'A Brief Guide to the British Royal Family by *The Crown*'s Historian Robert Lacey', *HistoryExtra*, 13 October 2020, https://www.historyextra.com/period/modern/why-royal-family-exist-guide-arguments-why-should-be-abolished-republicanism

10   'The Royal Touch: UK and British luxury brands receive boost from popularity of young royals', press release, Brand Finance, 25 October 2018

11   Carolyn Fiennes, 'Do Royals Help Charities? We're Finding Out',
     https://giving-evidence.com/2019/11/23, 16 July 2020
12   Philip Ziegler, *King Edward VIII,* Collins 1990: 107
13   Tom Nairn, *The Enchanted Glass*, Radius 1988
14   Tanya Gold, 'The British Monarchy Is a Game: Harry and Meghan
     Didn't Want to Play', *New York Times*, 15 August 2020
15   Hilary Mantel, 'Royal Bodies', *London Review of Books*, 21 February 2013
16   Frank Prochaska, *The Eagle and the Crown*, Yale University Press 2008:
     xii
17   Christopher Hitchens, *The Monarchy*, Chatto & Windus 1990
18   Jonathan Freedland, 'A Moment of Madness', *The Guardian*, 13 August
     2007
19   *Who Runs This Place?*, 343
20   'The Monarchy Is at Its Strongest in Years', *The Economist*, 19 May 2018
21   'The Cruellest Example Is Tom Bower', *Rebel Prince*, William Collins
     2018

# The dominions

1    D. Michael Jackson, quoting *The Globe and Mail* in Jackson (ed.), *The
     Canadian Kingdom*, Dundurn 2018: 15
2    Serge Joyal, 'The Oath of Allegiance' in *The Canadian Kingdom*, 148

# Getting rid of the Queen

1    Anne Twomey, 'Whitlam Wanted Palace to Interfere', *The Age*, 15 July
     2020
2    See Jenny Hocking, *The Palace Letters*, Scribe 2020
3    Paul Keating, *After Words*, Allen & Unwin 2011: 56
4    Mark McKenna, 'Waiting to Die?', in R. Aldrich, C. McCreery &
     A. Thompson (eds), *Crowns and Colonies: European Monarchies and
     Overseas Empires*, Manchester University Press, 2016
5    Citizens for a Canadian Republic, https:// https://www.canadian-
     republic.ca/goals.html
6    Benjamin T. Jones, *This Time*, Redback 2018: 14; 15
7    Malcolm Turnbull, *A Bigger Picture*, Hardie Grant 2020: 554
8    John Pesutto, 'COVID Bill a Test for Upper House', *The Age*, 30
     September 2020
9    'Bolger Sets Date for NZ Republic', *The Independent*, 22 October 2011
10   Don Watson, 'Rethinking the Republic', *The Monthly*, April 2019

11   Michael Kirby, '250 Years of the Crown in Australia: from James
     Cook to the Palace Papers (1770–2020)', *The Australian Law Journal,*
     November 2020

# The Commonwealth

1   *The Queen*, 466–69
2   Michael Wesley, 'Empire of Delusion', *Griffith Review* 59, 2017: 33
3   *The Empire's New Clothes*, 232
4   James Meek, 'The Two Jacobs', *London Review of Books*, 1 August 2019

# Spain and the transition to democracy

1   Paul Preston, *Juan Carlos*, Harper Collins 2004: 326
2   Tony Judt, *Postwar: a history of Europe since 1945*, Heinemann 2005: 521
3   David Jiminez, 'The Immoral Double Life of the Former King of Spain',
     *New York Times*, 13 August 2020
4   Nicholas Watt & Severin Carrell, 'Queen Hopes Scottish Independence
     Voters will "think carefully about future"', *The Guardian*, 15 September
     2014
5   'A Tarnished Crown', *The Economist*, 25 July 2020

# The Benelux countries

1   'Luxembourg Strips Monarch of Legislative Role', *The Guardian*, 12
     December 2008

# Asian monarchies

1   Prince Michael of Lichtenstein, 'The Role of Malaysia's King', 2 March
     2020, https://www.gisreportsonline.com/the-role-of-malaysias-
     king,politics,3105.html
2   Ben Anderson, *Imagined Communities*, Verso 1991:96
3   Herbert Bix, 'Emperor Hirohito's war', *History Today* 41:12, December
     1991
4   John Breen, 'The Quality of Emperorship in 21st Century Japan:
     reflections on the Reiwa Accession', *Asia-Pacific Journal*, 5 June 2020
5   John Berthlsen, 'Malaysia's Sultans Return to Power', *Asia Sentinel*, 19
     September 2014

6   Ahmad Hamid & Muhamad Ismail, 'The Monarchy and Party Politics in Malaysia', *Asian Survey*, Sept/Oct 2012: 946

7   See Eugenie Merieau, 'Buddhist Constitutionalism in Thailand', *Asian Journal of Comparative Law* 13, 2008: 302

8   Maisrikrod Surin, 'Learning from the 19 September Coup: advancing Thai-style democracy', *Southeast Asian Affairs*, Singapore 2007: 354

9   Puangchon Unchanam, *Royal Capitalism: wealth, class, and monarchy in Thailand*, University of Wisconsin Press 2020: 220

10  Duncan McCargo, 'Network Monarchy and Legitimacy Crises in Thailand', *The Pacific Review* 18: 4, December 2005

11  Soren Ivarsson & Lotte Isager, 'Introduction', *Saying the Unsayable: monarchy and democracy in Thailand*, NIAS Press 2010: 15–6

12  Pavin Chachavalpongpun, 'The Royalists Marketplace: the supply and demand for dissent in Thailand', *New Mandala*, 4 May 2020, https://www.newmandala.org/the-royalists-marketplace-the-supply-and-demand-for-dissent-in-thailand

## Transitional monarchies

1   James Traub, 'The Reform of the King', *Foreign Policy*, November 2012: 48

2   Roger Kershaw, *Monarchy in South-East Asia*, Taylor & Francis 2001: 159

3   Dhurba Rizal, *The Royal Semi-authoritarian Democracy of Bhutan*, Lexington 2015

4   Ursual Lindsey, 'Jordan's Endless Transition', *New York Review of Books*, 22 October 2020

## Why do they survive?

1   Ed West, 'Are We About to See the Return of the Kings?', *Spectator*, 24 May 2016

2   Bernard Yack, 'The Rationality of Hegel's Concept of Monarchy', *American Political Science Review*, September 1980: 709–20

3   Chris Rojek, *Celebrity*, Reaktion 2001: 198

4   Robert Aldrich & Cindy McCreevy, *Monarchies and Decolonisation in Asia*, Manchester University Press 2020: 9

5   Simon Jenkins, 'What's the Point of the Monarchy?', *Prospect*, 23 March 2011

6   Frank Prochaska, *Royal Bounty*, Yale University Press 1995, esp. 280–82

7    Eileen McDonagh, 'Ripples from the First Wave: the monarchical origins of the welfare state', *Perspectives on Politics* 13: 4, December 2015

8    *The Enchanted Glass*, 53

9    Zowi Milanovi, 'The Role of the Monarchy in the Netherlands', *In Defense of Marxism*, 13 May 2013

10   Paul Vaute, *Voie royale: essai sur le modèle belge de la monarchie*, Grâce-Hollogne, Mols, 1998: 85

11   'Exclusive Interview with Queen Margrethe II of Denmark', *Luxembourg Times*, 14 March 2012, https://luxtimes.lu/archives/31470-exclusive-interview-with-queen-margrethe-ii-of-denmark

12   Judith Brett, 'From Monarchy to Republic: into the symbolic void?', *Journal of Australian Studies* 47, 1996: 32.

13   Ernest Jones, 'The Psychology of Constitutional Monarchy', *New Stateman*, 1 February 1936

14   George Orwell, 'London Letter', *The Partisan Review*, Spring 1944

15   Quoted by Frederick Mount, 'The Importance of Being Ernie', *London Review of Books*, 5 November 2020

16   Christian Bjørnskov, 'Determinants of Generalized Trust: a cross-country comparison', *Public Choice* 130, 2007: 1–21

17   'The Times View on the Exile of Juan Carlos: reign in Spain', *The Times*, 4 August 2020

## Do we need a head of state at all?

1    'Sovereign Immunity', *The Economist*, 27 April 2019

2    *And What do YOU Do?*, 403

3    J. J. McCullough, 'Canada's Embarrassing Governor General Should Resign — and No One Should Replace Her', *Washington Post*, 18 August 2020

## A final note

1    Polls suggest falling support for a republic in Australia: see Jewel Topsfield, 'Support for a Republic Has Dived', *The Age*, 26 January 2021